Tennessee County History Series

TENNESSEE COUNTY HISTORY SERIES

Decatur County

by Lillye Younger

Joy Bailey Dunn
Editor

Charles W. Crawford
Associate Editor

MEMPHIS STATE UNIVERSITY PRESS
Memphis, Tennessee

Designed by Gary G. Gore

ISBN 0-87870-077-3

This volume is lovingly dedicated to my aunt, Mrs. Odell Freeman, who was instrumental in shaping my life, starting me to school in the primer at Hickory Grove School in Gibson County and later to Peabody High School in Trenton, Tennessee. She is understanding, kind, and generous. Without her encouragement and love this history might never have been compiled.

*D*ECATUR County anchors the middle of the extreme eastern edge of West Tennessee. Formed from Perry County in 1845, it is bounded on the north by Benton County and on the west by Henderson County. The Tennessee River, as it twists into a reverse ell, divides Decatur from Perry County on the east and from Hardin County on the south.

Situated midway between the two metropolitan areas of Memphis and Nashville, Decatur is a small county approximately 35 miles long and 15 miles wide at its most distant points. In 1849 a three-mile strip of land from Hardin County was added to the southern border of Decatur, making a total of 221,440 acres of forested hills and rich bottomland covering 346 square miles. Taking into account a huge bulge at the ankle, its outline loosely suggests the shape of a boot with its toe sticking in the southeast corner of Wayne County.

The land that was to become Decatur County was part of a strategic purchase made in 1818 by General Andrew Jackson and Governor Isaac Shelby of Kentucky. Representing the United States, Jackson and Shelby paid the Chickasaw Indians $300,000 for West Tennessee and West Kentucky, thereby opening up a vast new frontier for settlement. Following the transactions, the government sent five surveyors into West Tennessee to apportion it into five districts and to divide the districts into counties. The Lexington District, surveyed by Samuel Wilson, included Perry County, split by the Tennessee River.

The creation of Decatur County from Perry County stemmed from the inconvenience of having the county seat, Perryville, divided by the Tennessee River. In 1845, 200 citizens from the west side of the river, led by Samuel Brasher, petitioned for a new county. Consequently, the November session of the Tennessee General Assembly in that same year passed an act to form a new county

> out of that part of Perry County lying west of the Tennessee River to be known and distinguished by the name of Decatur in honor of and to perpetuate the memory of Commodore Stephen Decatur of the United States Navy, of whose services our nation should be proud and whose memory should be revered.

Commodore Decatur had won fame in the naval war with Tripoli and had later served with great distinction in the War of 1812.

The county lies at the eastern edge of the Plateau Slope of West Tennessee, a geologic province that stretches between the Mississippi and Tennessee rivers. Through millions of years, the successive forces of ocean, wind, and ice alternately built up and eroded this region creating a bedrock of dolomite topped with a thick layer of silt, sand, and loam making a very fertile plateau. Decatur County, bordering the Western Valley geologic formation which runs along the Tennessee River, also gained extensive limestone deposits from the sediment of shells and bones.

Fossil remains reveal a populous prehistoric marine life. Besides fish and shells there were giant turtles and huge reptiles of dinosaur size. In nearby McNairy County, the Coon Creek fossil bed has yielded evidence of ancient clams, oysters, and crabs along with a 40-foot skeleton of a mosasaur. Other fossils point to such exotic land animals as camels, prehistoric elephants, giant sloths, dog-sized horses, and saber-toothed tigers.

The natural forces that shaped the earth ages ago left Decatur County an interesting topography. The terrain is broken by gently sloping hills that flank long valleys. These hills distinguish the area from the flat table land that makes up most of the Plateau Slope. Standing 300 feet above the Tennessee River, they begin the gradual slope that ends with the 200-foot high bluffs above the Mississippi River.

Throughout the county a veinwork of streams drains the bottomland basins made fertile from ages of accumulated sediment deposited by river floods. The largest of the streams is Beech River named for the tremendous amount of beech mash that fell from the beech trees growing along its banks. The alluvial soil along these streams is dark and naturally suited for the growth of corn and other crops. Along the ridges the soil is much lighter, thinner, and sandy, excellent for pasture.

Decatur County offers not only beautiful landscape, but it also provides abundant natural resources. D. Craft, an early traveler recording in his diary impressions of the wilderness along the Ohio and Tennessee rivers on a voyage by steamboat from Pittsburgh to Florence, Alabama, took note of this beauty and made passing reference to the mineral riches as he described what later became the eastern boundary of the county:

> Cane grows along this part of the river in great abundance, from 25 to 30 feet high which looks most beautiful, having a clear stalk & a bunch of green blades or leaves just at the top. . . . Past (sic) more of the limestone rocks on the west side of the river. This ledge of rocks are full of round smooth holes, large enough for a person to enter in at, but are such a distance from the foot of the rocks that it would be impossible to ascend to them, except by a ladder. Those rocks look beautiful, being cover'd on top with scrubby cedars standing very thick & look very green.

The intriguing rock formations of which Craft wrote, while being one of the major distinguishing features of the county, also were visible evidence of valuable phosphate deposits to be dis-

covered later. Recognition of white phosphate was made first in
1896 along Tom's Creek in Perry County by prospectors familiar
with similar hard-rock phosphate from Florida. In 1901 an
extension of this white rock field was discovered in Decatur
County.

The county's phosphate deposits found in and at the top of
the limestone of the Silurian age, put there by chemical replace-
ment or secondary deposition by waters bearing phosphate derived from overlying phosphatic formations, lie in what are
known as the Beech River, Rushing Creek, and White's Creek
tracts. The Beech River tract extends from a point immediately
southeast of Parsons and runs in a southeasterly direction as far
as Decaturville. The Rushing Creek tract is situated about six and
one-half miles southeast from Parsons, and is separated from the
Beech River tract by a broad ridge. The White's Creek tract is
located about 12 miles southeast of Parsons and about three
miles from Bob's Landing on the Tennessee River.

In addition to phosphate, limestone is the source from which
several of the county's other mineral assets come. The limestone
itself is well suited for building materials, and also furnishes a
plentiful supply of high-grade gravel used for road construction.
When limestone is subjected to great heat and pressure, as it was
in Decatur County eons ago, marble results. Marble was mined
sporadically in the early years of the county, but rarely at all now.
There also exists a fine-grained sandstone, a cousin of limestone,
from which grindstones and whetstones are made.

Iron ore is another mineral that at one time was important to
the county. It led to a bustling industry centered around the
Brownsport Furnace. This area is now in the planning stages of
becoming a tourist attraction and is located in the area called
"The Old Coaling." The iron ore smelted in the furnace was a
heavy, brown material known technically as limonite.

The mineral wealth of Decatur County is matched doubly by
its wildlife. In the forests and canebrakes, game lives in almost
exotic abundance, now as much as when the Redman inhabited

the land. D. Craft, again writing in his diary, saw along the banks of the Tennessee River "hundred of wild fowls, flocks of beautiful green birds called 'Parrakeets,' and abundance of wild turkeys, screaming loons (fish eating birds), the Bald Eagle and Whip-porwill." This area was a favorite hunting ground for the Cherokee Indians where they stalked deer, birds, rabbits, and all types of smaller game and trapped for beavers, otters, minks, raccoons, panthers, and bobcats. Today the county is still considered to be a hunter's paradise.

The Indians and early settlers hunted their game in the tall, virgin forests that covered almost all of the county. It was and still is a timberland of upland hardwoods—red oak, white oak, tulip poplar, and hickory. Even today trees cover about 60 percent of the land area and continue to provide valuable lumber resources.

Amid the dense forests, the early settlers found rich farming land, especially along the banks of the Tennessee and the Beech rivers, as well as the smaller streams. A 200-day growing season made it worthwhile to clear land and plant crops. Today there are approximately 145,885 acres in farmland with a total of 906 farms, whose average is 161 acres. Cotton, corn, and grasses for pasture were the main crops grown in 1960; however, by 1975, soybeans had completely replaced cotton.

Decatur County is rich in land, trees, wildlife, and minerals, but perhaps its greatest resource is its people. With only 9437 inhabitants, according to the 1970 census, the county is not populous by the standards of many Tennessee counties, but neither does it have the traffic, crime, and pollution problems of metropolitan centers. The two largest towns are Parsons, with a population of 2167, and Decaturville, with a population of 958. And though more and more jobs are becoming available in the factories that continue to locate in the county, most of the residents still have roots deep in the land as did their ancestors, the hardy settlers who arrived in the nineteenth century and made communities.

Frontier Life

The first settlers of Decatur County were part of the cutting edge of that great westward movement of civilization across the North American Continent. Driven by a dream of a new life, strengthened by physical hardiness and strong iron will to endure peril and pain of hardship and privation, many settlers of Scots, Irish, and English descent moved in through the gateway of North Carolina. The process of westward movement occurred in efficiently repeated stages: entrance of the trailblazer-hunter-trader; displacement of Indians by treaty or force, or by both; acquisition and speculation of land; arrival of settlers who cleared forests for farms; initiation of trade resulting in the development of communities at key transportation points; establishment of towns; growth of business prosperity; and the creation of banks, industries and cities.

The area that is now Tennessee, in 1776, was considered as the western section of North Carolina. In 1777 that part was named Washington County. After the Revolutionary War, this land was made available in the form of land grants to war veterans. A private could receive 640 acres of land, a sergeant, 2000 acres, a captain, 3600 acres; comparable increases were alotted through the rank of general. The eastern portion of Washington County was more accessible to settlers at that time, and there were already thriving communities at Watauga and on the Holston and Nolichucky rivers. In 1796 the area west of the Tennessee River began to feel the white man's hand of development.

The purchase of West Tennessee in 1818 from the Chickasaw Nation by the United States Government started a steady flow of settlers into the area. The first settler of record in what was to become Decatur County was Jimmy Harris, who came to be known by the affectionate name of "Uncle Jimmy." At some time during the first decade of the 1800s, Harris paddled the Tennessee River and landed at the mouth of a little stream that he later named Cub Creek because of the numerous cub bears he had killed in that vicinity. "Uncle Jimmy" was of that intrepid breed of adventurer-hunter who traveled ahead of civilization.

Finding the lay of the land to his liking, he put down roots and waited for American civilization to catch up with him.

He did not wait long, for when Decatur was officially recognized as a county in 1845, approximately 300 people were living there. As in the development of a photograph negative, all parts of basic civilization quickly came into focus. The county was ideally situated for settlement; it could be reached by river as well as by land. Early immigrants found the arduous tasks of settlement eased somewhat by the towering poplars conducive for building; by hills which served as a protection against floods; by plentiful game for hunting, and fish; and by fertile bottomland for farming.

All the work involved in establishing a farm required many hands, so big families were the rule, often with as many as 12 to 14 children. It was typical for the men to work the fields and provide game for the table and for the women to do domestic chores. Many local residents still remember the weekly routine of frontier life endured by their grandparents. Keeping a home then was far different from now due to the conveniences provided by current labor-saving devices.

Clothes were washed not in a washing machine, but in a big black pot filled with water and heated by a fire. The clothes were rubbed clean on a brass washboard in large washtubs. Then they were boiled for awhile, rinsed several times, including once in blueing water. Next the clothes were hung to dry on a line or anything else convenient. In the summer the water from the washing was poured on the flower beds.

Since most clothes were handmade the value of care to prolong their use was great. Large families dictated the need for hand-me-downs. Besides normal deterioration, "bob" (barbed) wire fences were always around to snag and to tear clothing. Saturday was frequently spent by going into town. The farm housewife would see the latest products, styles, and fabrics, but usually could purchase only those things necessary. Sunday, of course, was the time for both religious and social activities held even if the church could not afford a full-time preacher. Following church, there was usually a big dinner for guests and relatives who came home with the family.

Frontier life was not easy, but essentially, it was peaceful, if drought, pestilence, or some other malady did not strike. The farm family was able to live a full life of simple well-being, with gardens for vegetables, cows for milk, steers for beef, hogs for pork and lard, chickens for eggs, and wild game for the killing. Farm life was a mode of existence that fostered stability and continuity, and a farm would stay in the same family for years. For example, Solomon Wyatt was granted 150 acres in Decatur County by the state of Tennessee in 1852. This same farm has been in the Wyatt family since that date, presently belonging to Mr. and Mrs. Lealon Wyatt, of Bath Springs. The Wyatt farm was the first farm in the county to be honored in the Farm Land Heritage Program in 1976, since it had been owned and continuously operated for over 100 years by the same family. Three other century farms also were honored: the Welch farm on Highway 69 where Weldon Welch now lives; the Keeton farm, operated by B. B. Keeton; and the Moore farm located near Decaturville on which Mr. and Mrs. Roy Moore live.

Any dreariness in frontier living was relieved by recreation in which everyone participated, unlike much of today's passive entertainment. There were quilting bees for the women, square dances for the young set, corn husking and log rolling for the men, and games such as mumble peg, horseshoes, and pitching dollars for the children.

At the square dances, partners danced to the calls of dosi-do and promenade. Ladies were usually clad in colorful calico dresses in shirtwaist styles with full skirts. Their partners were usually dressed in homespun clothing. Corn huskings were primarily for men. The contest was started when they were gathered at the barn. The man who shucked the most ears of corn in a given period of time was the winner. Log rolling was really more work than play. Logs were stacked high by hand, then rolled to the desired location.

Games were a common form of amusement for young as well as old. Due to the economic conditions, sometimes instead of pitching dollars it became necessary to pitch washers. Another game of interest was called "Jack Marbles." One big marble was placed with four smaller ones making a square around it. The object of the game was either to knock the "Jack Marble" out of the center first or to knock all five marbles out. This game interested the youth and also men, who played it in town as they waited for the livery stable man to hitch up a horse. Other popular games were "The Farmer in the Dell," "London Bridge is Falling Down," "Red Rover," "Go In and Out the Windows," and "Crack the Whip." These games were common in schools at recess and lunch hour.

Early Agriculture and Industry

The 1850 Census of Decatur County represented a picture in outline form of its bustling growth by listing the main occupations and the people who pursued them. It also provided their ages and state of origin. Some of this information is listed below:

Blacksmiths
George W. Tucker, age 48, North Carolina
John Jones, age 22, North Carolina
John Beaver, age 42, North Carolina
Alfred Haggard, 50, North Carolina
John Weaver, 22, Georgia
W. W. Herndon, 21, Tennessee
Gilbert McMillian, 66, North Carolina
Sampson Essary, 51, Tennessee
Elijah Goodnight, 41, Tennessee
Carroll M. Snodgrass, 18, Tennessee
Dempsey Veal, 80, Virginia
Joel Hensley, 37, Tennessee
Wiliam B. Herndon, 50, North Carolina
S. B. Campbell, 25, North Carolina
John Brazile, 53, North Carolina
Burriel Ivy, 31, North Carolina
Thomas J. Essary, 41, North Carolina
Nathaniel Moore, 62, North Carolina
John Olfin, 45, North Carolina
John McKnight, 39, Louisiana
J. W. Louis, 33, Tennessee
J. D. Louis, 25, Tennessee
Joseph J. Livingston, 25, Tennessee
Samuel Walker, 37, North Carolina
Nathan C. Davis, no date

Clerks
F. L. Fowler, 22, Kentucky
Sam A. Yarbro, 30, Tennessee
John C. Yarbro, 39, Tennessee
F. M. Bennett, 16, Tennessee
W. L. Morrow, 18, Tennessee
John A. Burrow, 22, Tennessee
Robert N. Hill, 27, Ireland
Thomas A. Noel, 38, Tennessee

Iron Masters
F. R. Lanier, 21, Tennessee
James A. Fall, 20, Tennessee

Manager
Henry C. Locket, 28, Tennessee

Constable
Hiram Haines, 42, North Carolina

Stone Masons
Edward Crane, 34, New York
H. A. White, 21, Tennessee
John M. Weaver, 44, Virginia

County Court Clerk
D. B. Funderburk, 45, South Carolina

Overseers
Thomas Fisher, 34, Illinois
William Wesson, 42, Virginia
John Thornton, 48, Virginia
Wm. T. Wesson, 29, North Carolina
H. H. Wesson, 37, North Carolina

Tanners
John Williams, 32, Tennessee
John L. Brasher, 22, Tennessee
William Stacy, 26, Tennessee
John Stacy, 22, Tennessee
Calmon Holy, 49, Virginia
James N. Hambleton, 28, North
    Carolina
Henry Eichor, 39, Pennsylvania
Harmon Tartomyon, 27, Germany
Frederick Gathart, 36, Germany
Alexander Walker, 15, Tennessee
Robert Raney, 28, Tennessee

Ferryman
John Turner, 69, Virginia

Tobacco Growers
Robert Campbell, 32, North Carolina
James Walker, 17, Tennessee
E. H. Reamey, 27, Virginia
Nathaniel A. Wesson, 24, North
    Carolina

School Teachers
Elias Jones, 30, North Carolina
Brian Peter, 40, Tennessee
Council Goodman, 48, North
    Carolina
C. M. Cotham, 33, Tennessee
Sam H. Kerr, 26, Tennessee
W. W. Shell, 21, Tennessee
Benj. H. Southerland, 31, South
    Carolina
Edward Morgan, 26, North Carolina
G. B. Rushing, 23, North Carolina
Thos. McMurray, 31, Tennessee
John B. Davidson, 41, Tennessee
Geo. W. Sawing, 29, Massachusetts

C. D. Hicks, 27, Tennessee
Jas. W. Lockwood, 24, New York
Andrew McGill, 30, Pennsylvania
Evan White, 43, Virginia

Wagon Maker
John Price, 54, North Carolina

Hotel Keeper
John W. Delany, 35, Tennessee

Trader
Ellis L. Roberts, 32, North Carolina

Tailors
John J. Jenkins, 43, Kentucky
Thomas M. Brown, 21, Tennessee
Jonathon Luton, 26, Tennessee
Anderson Smith, 38, Tennessee
Wm. H. Russell, 38, Kentucky

Carpenters
Joel L. Ashcraft, 42, North Carolina
L. G. Findley, 35, Tennessee
Jas. H. Watson, 50, Tennessee
Martin Clark, 42, Ireland
Jas. H. Moore, 35, North Carolina
Joab Wilson, 35, Tennessee
Calvin Westerman, 26, Tennessee
Abijah Veach, 47, Tennessee
Jahu Miller, 37, Tennessee
A. L. Moore, 34, North Carolina
H. W. Poor, 45, Georgia
Wade H. Shelby, 49, North Carolina
E. E. Pate, 25, Tennessee
Joseph Higgons, 51, South Carolina
Elisha Stevens, 32, Tennessee

Lawyers
William W. Dolton, 44, Rhode Island
A. Cummings, 30, Vermont
D. E. Mcrath, 34, North Carolina
J. M. Hill, 21, Tennessee
John I. J. Shelby, 24, Tennessee
John Bruce, 56, North Carolina
John McMillan, 27

Millers
Willie Jones, 58, South Carolina
Jacon Tucker, 57, North Carolina
M. W. Gale, 49, Virginia
William Walberton, 63, Virginia

Cabinet Maker
Jas. W. Gilberth, 41, North Carolina

Waggoner
Jeremiah Tubbs, 29, Tennessee

Doctors
Robert Keeton, 49, Illinois
J. H. Clardy, 24, Tennessee
Joel C. Hancock, 44, Tennessee
I. Smith, 32, Virginia
B. W. Raney, 35, North Carolina
Amos M. Yarbro, 32, Tennessee
Lawson Keney, 28, Tennessee
Henry C. Fryar, 43, North Carolina
G. H. Derryberry, 34, Tennessee
R. L. Gainus, 55, Virginia
John Parsons, 44, North Carolina
Joseph S. Douglas, 50, South Carolina
Wesly Doss, 41, Virginia
Samuel Hill, 80, Ireland
John Henderson, 44, North Carolina
Priar H. Smith, 33, Tennessee

Shoemakers
Thomas H. Oensly, 39, North
    Carolina
James Yarbro, 35, Tennessee
John H. McPhearson, 65, Scotland
J. W. Baker, 29, Alabama

Merchants
Thos. B. Garrod, 30, Alabama
C. H. J. Brisco, 26, Alabama
Paul H. Fisher, 28, Tennessee
W. H. Bennett, 24, Tennessee
Wm. H. Johnson, 29, Tennessee
Robert Young, 32, Pennsylvania
John Coats, 28, Tennessee
A. A. Shelby, 16, Tennessee
J. M. Pettigrew, 52, Ireland
Chas. S. Brodie, 48, South Carolina
J. B. Howe, 37, Kentucky
Jas. R. West, 28, Kentucky
Curry Pettigrew, 50, Ireland
H. Bradberry, 50, Ireland
William Martin, 23, Kentucky
John P. Nixon, Tennessee
Wm. Stout, 25, Scotland
U. T. Cole, 36, Tennessee
Thomas H. Peacock, 30, Tennessee
F. J. Pavatt, 34, Tennessee
E. J. Inglehart, 28, Maryland

Ministers
Phillip Ivy, 33, Tennessee, Methodist
John W. Fisher, 33, North Carolina,
    Methodist
Thomas Hay, 48, Ireland, Methodist
Priar Hill, 49, North Carolina, Baptist
S. M. Steed, 45, Georgia, Baptist
Hugh N. Rose, 51, Cumberland
    Presbyterian

Sheriff:
Hiram Lacy, 39, North Carolina

All of these activities showed that the pulse of the young county was strong and vital, but the lifeblood of the county was agriculture. With a 200-day growing season, abundant rainfall, and naturally drained, fertile bottomland for crops, the county was well suited for farming. Those wishing to farm came, acquired land, and built their homes with determination and hard work. They tilled the land, walking behind plows pulled by oxen or mules. They planted by hand, hoed weeds and grass, and nurtured the young plants. The "farmer's plight"—either hoping for more rain or for rain to stop—prevailed until crops were finally harvested in the fall. The family kept only what would be necessary for the winter and sold the rest.

Corn and cotton were the county's staple crops. Shelled, the corn fed livestock; ground, it made meal to feed the farmer. Cotton was the major money crop. For domestic purposes, it was carded and spun into cloth. The remainder of the crop was sold and shipped on the Tennessee River to waiting textile mills. The successful production of the cotton crop required gins. Transporting the cotton once it was picked was difficult in the early days of the county, and because of this, gins sprang up in several county localities—Parsons, Decaturville, Swallow Bluff, Scotts Hill, and Beacon.

The first cotton gin in Parsons, a roughly hewn two-story building constructed of yellow poplar with hand-planed bins and chutes, was operated by George Partin. This gin was located in the 100 block of the present Main Street, near McIllwain's Service Station. On one side of the building was a flour mill operated by R. F. Corklin. Partin later sold the gin and building to Adophus Rains. When Rains went out of business, Jim Lamping negotiated the sale to Hobart Goff. Goff razed the flour mill and rebuilt the gin in 1924. Some of the lumber from the sold flour mill was used in building his home at 217 Camden Road. Goff sold the gin in 1926 to White Brothers of Jackson. It burned in 1928. Will Long opened a cotton gin in Parsons in the late 1920s. It was located at the intersection of Goff Street and Tennessee Avenue, operated by Freeman Wilsons. Among the yearly residents who worked at the Parsons gins were Rube Ivey, Tom Hays, Ben Boyd, and Will Greer.

In 1935 H. D. Pevahouse operated a gin located in Decaturville city limits on Highway 69. In 1954 he sold it to John Austin, who sold it to Wayne Byrd. Bill Pratt earlier operated the gin in Decaturville. George Simmons operated the first cotton gin at Swallow Bluff in the late 1800s. He sold it to Charley Wilson in 1904. Later operators of the gin were Jess Boggan and Edd Lancaster. Lancaster later sold his interests to Boggan who continued operations until 1918. The gin was then purchased by G. C. Pollard and Hollis Hitchcock, who in turn sold it to Clint Tuten. H. D. Pevahouse operated the gin from 1924 until 1935. The last operator of the gin was Jahue Boggan, who continued the business until 1942.

The first gin in Scotts Hill was owned by Ephram Austin, one of the area's first settlers. Located at the rear of his mercantile store, it was a horse-powered gin. It produced a bale or a bale and one-half of cotton a day. Another gin at Scotts Hill was operated by Fate McKenzie and was located below the Austin Mercantile Company. Ed Austin also had a gin that was below the present site of the gymnasium. Another gin was on the grounds of the present livestock sale barn and was operated by John Pratt, and later by Tom Mitchell.

In addition to the gins for cotton, there were also grist mills for the corn. One of the earliest was Buckner Mill, located three miles south of Parsons on a hill overlooking Beech River. Built first on Bear Creek, James Edward Buckner had the mill moved to Beech River due to the lack of water. Jim Adair and W. G. Fonville helped construct the mill. They dynamited the rock wall in the bank of the river, letting the shaft down into the water. The shaft was connected to the small mill house perched on the bank and to the propellor resting above the riverbed. A dam was built across the river, backing up enough water to furnish power for the mill's operation. Two mill stones, located in the mill house, were attached to the shaft which was propelled by the force of the water.

Shelled corn was placed between the two stones and a lever tripped for grinding the corn into meal. The bottom mill stone had deep grooves cut into it and remained stationary while the other stone moved on top of it in a circular motion. The corn was crushed into corn meal and deposited into a hopper that could hold about five bushels of meal. The meal, when put in heavy canvas sacks, was called a "turn of meal." The payment was one-sixth of the corn ground. A square toll box was placed in the millhouse and the miller's share of the corn was placed in it. Money was not usually involved.

Drawing of gristmill.

The first grist mill in Scotts Hill was operated by Ephraim H. Austin and was located in a valley back of the present livestock barn. A dam was built to harness spring water and furnish power for the mill. Later, other grist mills were located there. Two mills were also located at Sugar Tree.

With the coming of gasoline-powered grist mills, business at the water propelled mills dwindled and operations ceased in the late 1930s. Erie Jordan of Parsons salvaged the cedar shaft from the Buckner Mill. The shaft furnished enough material to make both a cedar chest and a bed.

Unlike many other rural Tennessee counties, Decatur did not depend entirely on agriculture for its economy. It had been blessed by nature with valuable mineral deposits. One of these mineral resources which was important from the origin of the county was gravel. Created by the extensive limestone layers, the high-grade rocks were readily available. The first gravel pit in the county was situated at the foot of Parsons Cemetery and owned by R. H. Pentecost. He was also the first in the county to send a load of gravel to Shelby County.

Another early and interesting area industry was the mining of phosphate. The deposits were mined on the banks of Beech River and brought to Parsons by wagons for shipment by rail. The company was formed by T. S. Hughs of Clifton, Judge John A. Pitts of Nashville, and L. H. Burke of Parsons. It was incorporated for $3000 and was managed by L. H. Burke. The company owned mineral rights on the land for miles around including Wilkins Town and Taylor Town. The industry provided employment for county men, who received $1 a day. A man with a mule and wagon received $2.25 for ten hours work. The phosphate company was prosperous until the Panic of 1907. At that time, money available was aluminum and called "Lummox."

In 1904, Harry Burke had a one-ton block of phosphate at the World's Fair in St. Louis that won first prize. Preparing this stone was quite a feat. There were one dozen crosscut saws used, plus 100 pounds of sand paper, and 100 pounds of jeweler's dust. O. E. Buckner tended the saw, keeping the blades sharp. Tennessee is the only state in the Union that has a blue ribbon for phosphate.

Smiley Sand and Gravel Company, located near the Perryville Ferry at Perryville Landing in the late 1920s, was operated by Jack and Jim Smiley and their sister, Nell. The company was instrumental in supplying the necessary material for the construction of the Alvin C. York Bridge, as well as gravel for roads, vaults, and other bridges and sand for concrete in the construction of buildings.

Between 1846 and 1878, the iron deposits in Decatur County supported a prosperous iron smelting industry. The Brownsport Iron Company acquired 12,000 acres of land and built a clay brick furnace about 13 miles southeast of Decaturville. The great amount of land was needed to supply the ore and the trees needed to fire the furnace. Napoleon Hill of Memphis was the first president of the company and his associates were G. M. Trigg and C. P. Thornton.

Ore was dug out of the ground with picks and shovels by slave labor, and hauled by oxen-drawn wagons to the furnace where it was processed. The deposits were dumped into the top of the furnace and melted by the heat. A trough mold, about 1500 feet long, was built adjacent to the bottom of the furnace with smaller molds running horizontally to it. The trough mold was called "the sow" and the smaller molds that ran perpendicular to the trough were called "the pigs." It is from these names that a term "pig iron" was derived.

Liquid melted from the iron ore settled at the bottom of the furnace and ran out into the molds. While in the molten stage, as it began to cool, the liquid was "cut" from the main trough. The area surrounding the furnace was an inferno as the slaves worked cutting the iron apart from the main mold. The cooled pig iron was hauled to Brownsport Landing on the Tennessee River where it was shipped to foundries.

The fire was fed by oak wood, split into three and one-half foot-long sticks and placed lengthwise in a 50-foot circle. Leaves and brush were placed on the circle of sticks. All of it was then covered with dirt, forming a mound. This covering made it essentially air-tight, except for two air-holes. The fire was started at one opening in the bottom of the mound. The other opening, a draft hole, allowed the fire to breathe. When the wood began to burn, both holes were closed, allowing the fire to char rather than to reduce to ashes. After the wood had been charred, it was removed and used to fuel the furnace. The heat from this charcoal created no smoke, was more powerful than a wood fire, and lasted much longer.

On the furnace yard were powerful air bellows, operated by a steam boiler, which pumped air to keep the charcoal burning. The blaze inside the furnace was never allowed to go out. Because of this use of charcoal in manufacturing iron ore, the land in this area was known as "The Old Coaling."

A commissary was built to supply the laborers who lived nearby in log cabins. In later years this commissary was converted into a single dwelling. The late George Murphry of Parsons

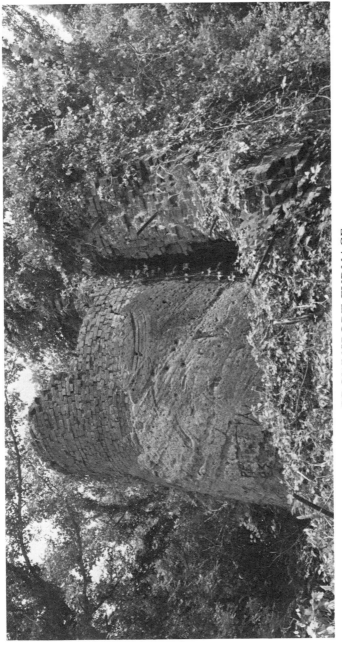

BROWNSPORT FURNACE.

This furnace was built in 1848. Iron was mined from nearby hematite deposits and processed here until 1878. The region is also known as "The Coalings," because of extensive charcoal production here during iron mining days.

recalled living there in 1938. At that time, he farmed this land
which then belonged to Tom Frank Hassell from Clifton.

The Brownsport Iron Company furnace operated successfully
for 30 years, but an extensive lawsuit developed that caused the
company to close in 1878. It was never re-opened. Today, beside
a quiet, abandoned rural road in a wooded setting, the ruins of
the Brownsport Furnace stand. The area is still known as "The
Old Coaling," and the Tennessee Historical Commission has
placed a marker recognizing the importance of the site on
Highway 100 which leads to the furnace.

Another gift from the county's mineral-rich land, one more
glamorous than phosphate mining and iron smelting, was that of
mineral water. Sulphur springs, their waters prized for medicinal
qualities, bubbled out of the ground at two places in the county—
Bath Springs and Sulphur Springs—giving rise for a time to a
healthy resort business.

William Hancock, a young doctor from North Carolina,
having just received his medical degree, was going west to seek
his fortune. Traveling in the vicinity of Bath Springs, he decided
to stop over to spend the night with a pioneer family about two
miles from Red House Stage Coach Inn. Inquiring about the
settlement where he was staying, he learned about 500 yards
from where he lodged was a number of sulphur springs. The
possibilities offered by the springs created a keen interest in him,
prompting him to establish his practice at Bath Springs.

As the area's population increased, business thrived, allowing
Dr. Hancock to build a 14-room, two-story log house with a rock
cellar. He opened it as a summer resort and offered mineral
baths, which he highly prescribed, to his guests. Bath houses also
were built near the five mineral springs. The sulphur water
proved to be good for the complexion since it did not have the
ingredient lime to clog pores. It was also a good tonic and was
recommended as a blood builder by the doctor. People came
from miles to be healed and entertained at the highly publicized
resort. Today there is no evidence of the once famous resort;
however, the sulphur springs are located on the Martin Landing
Road off Highway 114 which leads to the Clifton Ferry.

Another sulphur spring that once bubbled up in the center of the business area is located at the opposite end of the county near the Bible Hill Community. This thriving community had a big two-story hotel which was the headquarters for the many places to be healed of diverse diseases by the qualities of the sulphur water. This spring was encased by a wooden structure that had a shingle roof. The water bubbling out of the ground reflected various colors when struck by the sunlight. Primarily a summer spot, the hotel was named Sulphur Springs Health Resort. Dr. William G. Rains began his medical practice at this spring.

One natural resource of which the county has always had an abundance is trees. The great stretches of upland hardwoods— white oak, red oak, tulip poplar, and hickory—have been a haven for sawmills, which were found in every community. Arthur Evans was a widely known sawmill operator who lived in Parsons, as was John Pratt from Scotts Hill. Working for John Pratt were Joe Taylor, Shack Davis, and the Taylors—Mack, Charley, Virgil, and Ernest. Lowell Pratt operated a sawmill in the Cozette Community and Delmar Ballinger operated a sawmill near Bawcum Cemetery. Ballinger's father, Dock Ballinger, operated sawmills at various places, including Ballinger's School, Yellow Springs, and Sugar Tree. Stanley Gulledge operated a sawmill in the Prospect Community.

In addition to industries derived from the county's natural resources, several miscellaneous manufacturing ventures existed earlier. A heading factory was owned by a Parsons from French Lick, Indiana, in the early days of Parsons. This factory made heads, or ends, for barrels. It was located near the present Decatur County Hospital. A bedspring factory was operated by R. L. Snyder, located in Parsons around 1904. G. W. Partin owned a hoop factory also in Parsons at this time.

As new communities in the county developed, their needs grew for necessary service establishments such as blacksmith shops and livery stables. Blacksmiths who lived in Sugar Tree were Tom Bates, John Farlow, and Bill Terry. Claude Dillinger moved to Perryville from Indiana and established a blacksmith shop in 1897 and Nathaniel Moore had a shop at Sardis Ridge.

Jim Lyles ran a blacksmith shop in Parsons back of the Rustic Theater on Main Street. Anthony Fisher operated a shop near the railroad water tank and Dee Hall had one back of Maxwell's Department Store on Long Street. Lee Stone's shop was on the Bible Hill Road and, after his death, was operated by his son Terry. John William Smith, in his late 80s, currently operates a shop at Cedar Hill.

Livery stables were a necessity long before motor drawn vehicles arrived in the county. The livery stable was a building where horses were for hire, along with buggies, rigs, hacks, and surreys. Drummers, now called salesmen, came to town via train and would hire a rig to call on their customers in nearby towns. The livery stable also served as a parking lot. When a rider would leave his conveyance at the livery stable, the attendant would take the horse out of harness, water and feed it, and keep it until the owner returned. The usual charge was $2 for the full-day's parking.

The livery stable in Parsons was owned by J. K. Pettigrew and was located on the east side of Main Street, across from Virginia Avenue. Pettigrew, born in Decatur County on June 13, 1844, returned from the Civil War to resume his mercantile business at Oak Grove. A year later he opened a branch store at Sulphur Springs. Pettigrew also operated a livery stable from 1897 until 1907, at which time he moved to Sulphur Springs. The Pettigrews lived in a two-story house built north of the store.

G. W. Partin also owned a livery stable in Parsons that was operated by Will Fonville. In 1907 Will Rains and E. J. Houston opened and operated a livery stable across the street from Pettigrew's. They operated the business until 1911 at which time, it was sold to B. F. McClannahan of Scotts Hill. B. Lewis built a stable in 1916 at the time when untamed western horses were being shipped to the county from Texas. His business was located at 113 Tennessee Avenue, but later moved to what is now 117 Tennessee Avenue South.

Bob Laster went into partnership with S. L. Jennings after the Lewis business closed. The manager of their stable was Jess Houston. By this time keen competition forced Tom Hayes to put in still another livery stable on Fourth Street. There was also a livery stable located in connection with Smith Hotel in Decaturville. Eventually, the livery stable—a symbol of an age—vanished.

Depression and Economic Recovery

By the turn of the century, the economy of the county, based mainly on agriculture and aided by the products of its natural resources, was stable and slowly growing. The Decatur County Bank, the first bank in Decaturville, was chartered on September 23, 1889, with a paid capital of $5000. The first bank opened in Parsons in 1903 as the Bank of Parsons with a captial stock of $25,000. Four years later the Farmers Bank, also in Parsons, began business capitalized at $20,000.

However, the stock market crash of 1929 was a national catastrophe that touched every section of the country. Banks were forced to close. Debtors were unable to pay their loans. Panic erupted and a disastrous economic depression set in. The Bank of Parsons folded in 1931. The suspension of all bank operations for four days by President Franklin D. Roosevelt in 1933 closed the Farmers Bank and the Decatur County Bank. Both banks re-opened, however, and the Farmers Bank in Parsons was reported to be the first to do so in Tennessee.

Many farmers who had mortgaged their farms lost them. Cotton sold for $25 a bale. Corn brought 50¢ to 60¢ a bushel. Peanuts sold for 4¢ a pound. A thousand-pound steer brought only $50, and a 200-pound hog went for $2.80 to $4.

Although the government later sent commodities to Decatur County that were distributed by the American Red Cross to the needy, most of the people of the county were fortunate in that they had always depended heavily on homegrown necessities. Consequently, they could live off the land in pioneer fashion. When hunters were not able to buy shotgun shells for 60¢ a box, they trapped animals for food. Streams were seined for turtles and fish to eat. Salads were gathered from the woods, including wild "poke sallet," narrow and broad leaf dock, creasy, wild turnip salad, lettuce, rabbit ear, and dandelions. In the fall hickory nuts, walnuts, and hazelnuts were gathered and black-berries furnished jellies and jam.

Conditions became so bad that some families had only stock peas to cook in clear water without any seasoning. Others lived on parched corn for days. Everyone tried to keep a cow for milk and butter, even people who lived in towns.

Wood and coal were the chief heating products. Farmers cut their own wood, selling some to their town neighbors for $1 a rick (a stack eight feet long and four feet high). Coal sold for $3.60 a ton and laborers received 50¢ per day to haul and unload an order of coal. Wage for farm laborers was 25¢ per day. Farmers paid 35¢ per 100 pounds to have cotton picked. Local farmers usually swapped labor, helping each other on the farm. Clerk hire was $1.50 per day by 1933 and 1934.

Low wages were matched by low prices for staple products. Two pounds of coffee sold for 35¢ and a 24-pound sack of flour cost 59¢. Meal was 24¢ for a 24-pound bag. Soup beans sold for 5¢ per pound.

With the successful policies of President Roosevelt's "New Deal," the national economy began a slow recuperation and the hardships of the Great Depression eased gradually. In Decatur County, a welcome sign of economic recovery occurred on April 11, 1938, when Salant & Salant, Incorporated, opened its plant in Parsons to manufacture men's work shirts.

The plant started the first day with five machine operators: Lima Houston, Dorothy Keeton, Jettie Murphy Tillman, Rada Thomas, and Mary Joe Stone. By the end of 1938 the work force had increased to about 50, and the payroll for the first year was $28,000. Despite low wages, partially due to the workers' un-familiarity with the new machines and to being paid by piece-work, the plant was a healthy addition to the county, and has grown healthier.

Located at 706 Tennessee Avenue South—the name now changed to Salant, Incorporated—the plant employs about 650 people and has operated continuously since its inception except

Farmers Bank in Parsons, 1929. *Left to right,* Wess Jennings and Joe Jennings.

Opening the new building of Farmers Bank in 1954. *Left to right:* H. D. Pevahouse of Decaturville; Hugh Hicks of Jackson, president of the Tennessee Bankers Association, cutting ribbon; Hobart Townsend of Parsons.

for a three-month period in 1940. Harold White came to Parsons as superintendent of the plant when it opened and served continuously until January 30, 1970. He was succeeded by Gerald Hughs who is presently serving in this capacity. The first mechanic was Jimmy Burns and the first office employee was Eulene Latta. Marjorie Barnette Brasher was the first floor lady and had charge of the sewing room. Bert Baker was the driver of the first transfer truck. When the plant first started, Joe Lipshie, now chairman of the board of directors in the New York office, did all the cutting. In 1942 Francis Holman and Donald Bangs served in this capacity. W. T. Veasey headed the Atlas department with Gene Shaw as the first shipping foreman and Wynema Myracle as the first personnel director.

The success of Salant, Incorporated, helped to bring other industry to Decatur County. In 1959 Kaddis Manufacturing Corporation, with home offices in Rochester, New York, located at 710 Florida Avenue South in Parsons. The plant produces precision screw machine parts. Harold Riker served as the plant's first manager. Dick Prinsen replaced Riker, who died January 14, 1969. At this time, Thomas Baker and Thomas Cotham were promoted to assistant plant managers. In 1965-1966 the size of the building was doubled to 36,000 square feet, and in 1970 an additional 5000 square feet were added. Beginning with only six employees, the plant now employs 104.

The Decaturville Sportswear Company, Incorporated, manufacturers of women's sportswear, started its Decaturville operation on September 9, 1960, and was a boost to the county seat's economy. It began operation in the old Decaturville gymnasium, made available to the company by the town of Decaturville, the Decatur County School Board, and the Decatur County Court. In the beginning, the plant personnel numbered less than 100.

Four expansions, totaling 178,000 square feet, boosted the plant's area to 196,000 square feet. In 1968 they expanded to 256,000 square feet at an estimated cost of more than $500,000. Largo Road was closed when the two-floor addition was constructed to house a lunchroom-cafeteria, administrative offices, storage space, and restrooms. At the time, the new addition boosted to 1600 the number of employees; however, today the total is only 800. The first plant manager was Louie Carnie. In 1967 he was replaced by Ray Rindone, and he in turn by Lloyd Anderson. Those who have served as personnel director were Ray Rindone, Lerah Washam, Swan Pollard, and presently, Rebecca Adams. The Decaturville Sportswear Plant had been financially instrumental in the construction of numerous houses in the city, as well as in the stimulation of additional places of business. The plant has provided employment for not only those in Decatur County, but also for surrounding counties.

Thermo Dynamics, Incorporated, producer of commercial refrigerators, located at Parsons in 1962. The first plant manager was Hugh Lasater. The number of employees in its beginning was 30 and today there are 150 with a payroll over $1,000,000. The first office manager was Joe Beuhler and the first office employees were Martha Tyler and Sue Scott. Billy Goff was also an early employee. Billy Bedingfield was the company's first foreman. The present plant manager is Jim Ferguson and foremen are Don Armstrong, Edd Brumfield, Donnie Cook, Larry Fisher, Thomas Howers, Don McCorkle, and Rudolph Paul. Heads of various departments are Nick Wulfert, material control manager; Clay Blankenship and Carl Daniel, maintenance managers; John Freligh, production control; William Gilchrist, engineer manager; Lucille Keeton, accounting manager; Jack Mills, controller; and Don Tinto, quality manager.

Kol-Pak Industries, makers of commercial refrigeration, located in Crowder Industrial Park at Decaturville in 1968. Founders of the plant are Douglas Hayes, James Smith, and Jack Dalton. Employing six people in the beginning, the plant presently has 250 workers. It has expanded until now there are plants located in Parsons, Decaturville, Lobelville, and Scotts Hill. The corporate headquarters for all the plants is Parsons. The company acquired Norris Dispensers in 1971, makers of milk dispensers and beverage coolers. The Scotts Hill plant is manufacturer of the McCall Division. The refrigeration division manufactures walk-in and reach-in freezers and coolers and refrigerated warehouses.

Jack Dalton is president of the company and plant managers are Don Moore, Frank Cunningham, Jerry Graves, and Ronnie Moore. Blair Stenz is general manager and Joe Jetton is sales manager. Comptroller is Gaylon Yates and purchasing agent is Charles Wortham. Traffic manager is Billy Goff and office manager is Jim Shaw.

The plant has 250,000 square feet of floor space and employs 15% females and 85% males. Presently, there are two shifts employed at Lobelville, located in Perry County. Scotts Hill is the latest plant having opened in 1975 and is housed in the headquarters of the former textile plant on Main Street. The Parsons plant is located in Parsons Industrial Park on Ninth Street. A large amount of money is distributed in the county from the payroll of these plants.

The newest plant to locate in the county is Karlyn Manufacturers in 1970 at 207 Tennessee Avenue South in Parsons. Makers of jeans, the plant changed names in 1974 to Commodore Apparel. This plant is one of six located in Tennessee with headquarters in Nashville. The first plant manager was Katie Rushing; Bill Harden now holds that position. Carolyn Patterson was the first floor lady; present employees working in that capacity are Mrs. Dean Coats and Hazel Milam. The first office worker was Brenda Funderburk, who has continued in that position. Thirty-five people were employed the first year and the present total employment is 90.

As new industry moved into the county, the natural resources continued to be utilized. Tinker Sand & Gravel Company, situated at the landing where the ferry once operated, came to Perryville in 1938. The company employs 15 and has been in continuous operation except for several years during World War II. The latest sand and gravel company is the Teague Brothers Company, which also employs 15.

In 1957 an open limestone operation, known as Western Materials, was begun near the Jeanette Community by N. J. Boogie on Highway 69. In May of 1966, Western Materials moved away and Vulcan Materials Company—Mid-South Division moved in. There are 25 employees at the mine and the

annual payroll is approximately $130,000. The company con-
tracts agricultural lime and road rock to companies who sell in
West Tennessee. The mine produces around 1,000,000 tons a
year.

Although industry was making great contributions to the
economy after the Depression, farming continued to be the
mainstay of Decatur. Improved agricultural methods led to rising
yields per acre and higher prices for farm products resulted in
more money for the farmer. For cotton, the yield increased from
.39 bales per acre in 1879 to one bale per acre in 1959. The
average yield of corn in the county in 1952 was 21 bushels per
acre; in 1965 it was 52 bushels, and in 1975 the average had
increased to 60 bushels per acre.

Cotton and corn maintained their place as major crops in the
county through 1960. For some years before then, however,
cotton had been declining in number of acres planted until in
1975 it had been entirely replaced by soybeans. Two main
reasons perhaps account for this decline. The first is that the
production of cotton became less profitable. The second is that
more farmers found jobs in factories and thus became part-time
farmers planting soybeans, which require much less time and
maintenance than cotton. Much of the arable land also came to
be used as pasture for livestock.

Livestock production continues to be the largest source of
income in the county with 60 percent of the farm income coming
from it. Hogs are the largest single source of livestock income,
averaging 33 percent. Cattle provides 26 percent of this income,
with sheep and dairying providing the remainder.

The Scotts Hill Auction Company is a well-established market
for livestock. It holds weekly sales and furnishes an outlet for
cattle, hogs, sheep, and goats. Tom Mitchell started the sale barn.
Later, Youel Gibson joined him as a partner, and at Mitchell's
death Henry Gibson bought part interest.

Another boon to the area's farm economy occurred in 1960
when a hog buying station was started in Decaturville. Within the
first six years the operation put more than $10,000,000 into the
pockets of area farmers. Built by Wayne Byrd, the building was
leased to Armour & Company. In 1975, Morrell Packing

Company leased the building and it sold to William Mac Johnson. The first buyer at the station was Herman Hayes. Other buyers include Joe Akin and Paul White. Orbin McPeake is presently serving as hog buyer.

Pines have been set on land not suitable to row crops and pastures. In 1964, 47 farmers planted 172,000 pine seedlings as compared to 141,500 planted by 40 farmers in 1963. Tree farms service a steady, though small, lumber industry. Overcutting, grazing woodlands, and improper selection have caused some problems in efficient and profitable land use.

A different kind of "farming" began in Decatur County in 1968 when Robie Dodd experimented with catfish in six managed lakes. At harvest time his lakes were drained, the catfish deposited into huge vats, and the fish sold. Bill Benedict is now owner of those lakes. Catfish lakes prove profitable as well as recreational since they are open to the public for fishing at a small price per pound of fish. Owners of other area catfish lakes are Terry Reid who has six big lakes located near Bear Creek, Lewis Lacy who has two lakes in Garrett Community, Troy Brasher who has a lake near Lost Creek boat dock, John D. Vise, Mack Chandler who has a number of small lakes, Troy McCormick, and Chunk King who has a lake near Perryville.

Decatur County holds the record for the world's largest blue catfish which was caught by Joe Potts in October of 1971 in the Tennessee River. The channel cat tipped the scales at 112 pounds, measured 53½ inches long and 38 inches in girth. The distance between the eyes measured eight inches.

Another source of income in the county is musseling on the Tennessee River. Not only is it a way of life, but it is a profitable occupation. Shell buyers employ diggers who are paid by the number of pounds of mussels they catch. Many have been known to earn $25 to $40 a day, working an average of eight hours.

The early method of musseling was with equipment made from iron pipes and wires, called brails, which were lowered from boats and raised by hand. The more modern method is to raise the brails by the outboard motors on the boat. When the brails are lowered to the river bottom mussel beds, the mussels clamp down on them, and are hauled up. A new method for catching the mussels uses scuba divers who hold a basket in one hand and pick up mussels with the other and bring them to the surface.

Mussel shells are shipped to Japan where they are used in the cultured pearl industry. Buttons are also a product from mussel production. Buyers at Perryville from time to time include Edd Lee, Dave Stafford, Dan Eugene McFall, and Bernard Lee.

The river provides another job market—the towboat industry —for Decatur Countians. About 150 people, male and female, work on the towboats which ply the Tennessee, Ohio, Mississippi, Green, Cumberland, Missouri, and Illinois rivers.

Since the Depression, and the county's growing industrialization, traditional patterns in employment have changed with an increasing number of women working outside the home. Women have exchanged full-time homemaking roles for employment as production workers, clerks, grocery store checkers, school bus drivers, political officials, and machine shop laborers. More than 2000 county women are employed in the industrial plants, working alongside men, and successfully performing the same tasks.

Robie Dodd at fish pond.

From the dire straits of the Depression, the economic recovery of Decatur County has been steady, sure, and solid. Per capita personal income grew from $7895 in 1960 to $11,842 in 1975, an average above much of the South. With its natural resources, productive land, and willing workers for industry, the county's economic future has solid possibilities of being bright.

Religion and Churches

The early settlers of Decatur County might have brought with them only meager belongings, but they were never short of religious faith. Oftentimes faith was the only thing they had to keep them going, and they clung to it with the same steadfastness and tenacity that they used in overcoming the hardships of a wilderness to create a civilization. In the beginning of every community one of the first orders of business was to establish a church. Since the majority of the people coming into the frontier were protestants, the denomination of the church was assured to be either Presbyterian, Baptist, or Methodist.

Even though the Presbyterians had an early start, the Baptists and Methodists grew more rapidly with the influx of new settlers. With each church being independent and autonomous, and no insistence on educated ministers, the Baptist denomination was well suited for frontier conditions. The growth of the Methodist denomination can be largely attributed to the success of the circuit riders who spread Methodism throughout the wilderness. These horseback preachers rode from community to community putting up at anyone's house where they were made welcome and preaching the gospel in brush arbors, barns, under a tree, or, rarely, in a church. Aside from the Bible and other books, they carried little as they traveled the countryside. From the work of these circuit riders stemmed the "camp meetings."

On the frontier, the church was frequently the social and educational center of settlement life as well as spiritual meeting place. The camp meetings and all day preaching with dinner on the ground were not only fervent religious events but also social occasions of happy fellowship. Furthermore, many of the early churches served as school houses during the week.

The development of churches in Decatur County followed essentially the pattern that had been set in the earlier frontier sections of Tennessee. In 1887 the principle denominations in the county were Missionary Baptists, Methodist Episcopal South, and Cumberland Presbyterian. Though in new buildings, many of the churches that supported these denominations still exist.

Most of the Missionary Baptist churches in Decatur County belong to the Beech River Baptist Association. This association, meeting at the Union Missionary Baptist Church in Chesterfield, was established in October of 1870. The first delegates appointed to serve at that 1870 convention were R. R. Dennison, W. M. Bray, and E. H. Walker. The association includes churches in Henderson, Chester, and Decatur counties.

Churches in the association in Decatur County to date are Bible Hill, Bath Springs, Beacon, Bear Creek, Bunches Chapel, Calvary, Cub Creek Hall, Decaturville First, Hopewell, Lone Chestnut, Mt. Zion, New Chapel, New Hope, Parsons First Baptist, Perryville First Baptist, Salem, Tomlin Chapel, Sardis Ridge, and Parsons Southside. Parsons First Baptist Church was admitted to the association in 1889.

Thurman Creek Primitive Baptist Church

Thurman Creek Primitive Baptist Church was established July 27, 1833, in a log building. At the time, it was in Perry County since Decatur was not established until 1845. The three acres for the church building came from the H. B. Kelly farm, located 11 miles south of Decaturville. Like so many of the early churches, it served as both church and school for the community. Serving as the first deacons were Temple Hicks, Elias Deaton, and William Woolverton. There was a membership of 13.

In 1912 a new weatherboarded building was constructed about half a mile from the first building on the Brooxie Thompson Road. This building served the members until 1973 when a brick veneer building was constructed. The new building is approximately 36 x 50 feet with a concrete block basement which houses a kitchen. It is a beautiful modern building located in a picturesque section of Decatur County. Present deacons serving the church are Lealon Wyatt, Rural Brigance, and Nathan Maness and the pastor is Priddy Smith of Henderson, Tennessee. The total membership presently is nine.

Bear Creek Baptist Church

Perhaps the oldest Missionary Baptist Church in Decatur County dates back to 1842, three years before the county was organized. It is located one mile west of Parsons on the old freight line road on land deeded by Matt Houston. The church received its name from the community it serves. Pioneer families from North Carolina and Virginia noted the large number of bears living in the cane thickets near the creek bank and named the little settlement "Bear Creek."

The original church building was a log structure about 300 yards from the present building at the old meeting spring. Used for a church and school, it was located near the present home of Olan Houston.

The second building was located at the present spot and also was of logs. In 1902, S. M. Houston bought the building when the members voted to build a new church. He moved it and used it for a barn. The third building was a frame structure and also was used as a public school for a number of years. The church outgrew the building and in 1945, the present building was constructed. Its outer walls are made from Decatur County limestone rocks. The early church records date to August of 1842. L. M. Stead was clerk at this time and James K. Hall moderator. The first roll reveals 51 males and 51 females dated from 1842 to 1953. The ledger lists males on one side of the page and females on the other.

Conference meetings were held monthly and each time members were added to the fellowship. Some pioneer members listed were Lastima Houston, Sam Rains, Edmon Pettigrew, Isaac Rains, Calvin Watson, Austry Hays, Daniel Brown, A. C. Rains, Henry Myracle, and 11 slaves, male and female. Others included Jacob Conder, Polly Bray, Samuell Bray, Catheryn Wilson, Harvey Fedda, and Maude Turner.

In October of 1842 a camp meeting was held near the old meeting spring and lasted two weeks. People from far and wide came and camped for the protracted meetings. In December of 1842, it is recorded that the members of the fellowship "met in peace." It was moved and seconded to choose deacons. Issac Rains and B. Graves were chosen. One entry reveals that in July of 1848 the church did not meet because of smallpox in the neighborhood. One of the early pastors mentioned was T. W. Stark. He was chosen by request of the association of four churches, to unite them. They paid him $150 a year to spend all of his time with the four churches. They agreed to pay $25 at Bear Creek and more "if it was cold." In 1849, the church chose Balcom Rains as deacon. In 1850 M. P. Green was called to state whether he would serve as pastor. He accepted and was duly installed, the church pledging to sustain him so long as he sustained the scripture.

Several members were expelled for having moved from the bounds of the church without calling for letters. Other members had charges brought against them for dancing and gambling and their names were withdrawn.

On November 19, 1923, Joe Jennings was elected pastor of the church. It was voted to pay the pastor's salary in monthly payments. Records show that on April 8, 1923, his salary was $3.35 for that Sunday. A revival dated August 8, 1926, was held by G. G. Joyner of Beggs, Oklahoma. He received $46.42 for his services. Later, he was elected as pastor of the church.

Others who have served as pastor are Bob Pettigrew, W. A. Moody, and Floyd Rogers. The present pastor of the church is Wayne Vernon. Under his leadership the church has erected a parsonage, which was completed in 1973 near the church.

New Hope Baptist Church

The six-acre building site for New Hope Baptist Church was deeded by John S. Sullivan in 1848. The church covenant was written and signed September 24, 1842, with 86 charter members. E. Blount was the first clerk with L. M. Stead the first moderator and the first pastor until February of 1848. Among the charter members were E. Blount, Asa Rushing, James Lomax, Stephen Moody, William Myracle, William Griffin, John Bartholomew, James Deere, Elizabeth Myracle, Riley Johnson, Leroy Moore, Greenbury D. Rushing, and Jacob Smith.

E. Washburn served as the second pastor. The first Sunday School was organized in 1851. The church closed in 1902; however, it was reorganized on September 20, 1914, with 30 members. Sam Tolley served as clerk and W. F. Boren as pastor.

J. W. C. Gibson served as superintendent of the Sunday School for 31 years and as deacon until his death in January of 1974. G. W. Ward was elected clerk in 1918 and served until 1959. He also served as deacon and adult Sunday School teacher until his health failed. Willie H. Tillman was elected as clerk in 1959 and served until 1963.

The church went to half-time preaching in 1953 with J. V. Reeves serving as pastor. He served until 1956. Myracle Ward was elected clerk in September of 1963. Silas Smith served as pastor of the church from 1961 until his retirement August 19, 1973.

Jeff Flowers was called to serve the church in November of 1973 and in January of 1974 the church returned to full-time preaching. The present pastor is Bunis Smith. Louise Tolley has served as secretary and treasurer for the past 26 years.

Bath Springs Baptist Church

Dr. J. F. Hancock, founder and early doctor at Bath Springs, was instrumental in erecting the First Baptist Church in Civil War days. The one-room, log church-school combination was erected across Highway 114 from the Dr. B. M. Brooks home.

Later, around 1880, the building was torn down and a yellow poplar building was built on Dock Davis' land near the present Baptist Church. It too served as a church-school combination. In 1913, Dr. B. M. Brooks donated the land which was located about 150 feet from the former building, and a church-school building was built, replacing the earlier one. This combination served until 1929 when a new consolidated school was built in the community. Joe Jennings, who was pastoring the church at the time, bought the building, to be used as a church only, and the land and gave it to the congregation. Later in 1959, a modern block building was constructed.

Cub Creek Hall Missionary Baptist

The Cub Creek Hall Baptist Church was organized in 1890 as the New Pleasant Ridge Church. The name was changed later to Cub Creek Hall Church for the community in which it was located. The original one-room, log building was located just across the highway from the present church.

John Quinn gave the land for a new two-story building several years later. The lower floor was used for church services and a school. The upper floor was used for the Cub Creek Masonic Lodge. In 1961 a new one-story building was erected. The oldest minutes to be found report that the church held the 55th session of the Beech River Baptist Association in 1925. Among the early preachers who served there were A. U. Nunnery, W. H. Hooper, Nick Duke, and Clarence Mullins. Donald Bain was elected pastor in 1976.

New Prospect Missionary Baptist Church

New Prospect Missionary Baptist Church's first building was a log structure thought to have been built in the late 1700s; however, no date has been found. It was located in the north end of Decatur County near the Henderson, Benton, Carroll county

lines called "County Corner." In later years the log building was
torn down and a one-room boxed building was erected. This
served the congregation until 1966 when a modern brick building
was built.

The Southwestern District Missionary Baptist Association was
held at this church in 1851 according to an old minute book.
Among the pastors who have served here were Clarence Mullins,
Woodard Bartholomew, and A. U. Nunnery. The present pastor
is Holland Campbell who was elected in 1976.

Hopewell Baptist Church

Hopewell Baptist Church was organized on August 5, 1900,
as recorded in its first written record. Old settlers say services
were held in a one-room, log house close to the present church
site before that date. The first pastor according to written records
was J. B. Hayes. J. R. Lunsford was elected first church clerk and
among the first deacons were W. T. Rhodes, Bill Goodman, and
T. J. Ashcraft. Other pastors who have served the church include
W. M. Wood, Alvis Moore, Z. R. Overton, T. J. Park, C. V. Jones,
T. H. Boyd, Richard Rogers, W. L. King, A. U. Nunnery, C. L.
Haggard, G. G. Joyner, J. R. Todd, Silas Smith, Donald Franks,
Eamel Broadway, and G. C. Roper, Jr.

Sardis Ridge Baptist Church

Sardis Ridge Baptist Church was an early church in Decatur
County, constructed of logs and located west of the present
church. There were only three other churches in the county at the
time of its organization.

An early settler, W. Calvin Cole came to Tennessee in 1866
from Randolph County, North Carolina, and bought a tract of
land now known as the Crowell place. He and his wife, Clarrisa,
gave five acres of land for the Sardis Ridge Church and cemetery

on July 17, 1884. The log church was torn down and a new church built which was used for both church and schoolhouse.

Ministers were Reverend Parsons, John Thomas, and Reverend Holloway. Among the school teachers who taught at the school were Jack Moore, Vernon Striegel, Jula McMurry, and Eva Hays. Ministers serving this church were Joe Jennings, Grant Tomlin, G. G. Joyner, Silas Smith, and Gant Rushing.

In 1966 a new building was constructed of concrete blocks with a basement for Sunday School rooms. The first service was held in this building on May 15, 1966, with Roy Rushing of Jackson as pastor. The church has an enrollment of 50 and the present pastor is Nelson Renfroe.

First Baptist Church, Parsons

The First Baptist Church in Parsons was organized in the "Big Parlor" of the home of Mary Buckner. Charter members were Mary Buckner, Clemmie Coggins, Ike Buckner, Ollie Buckner, Mamie Buckner, Anna Fonville, W. G. Fonville, David Fonville, Mr. and Mrs. Edd Gooch, and Jack Riggs. The first pastor was Nick Duke.

From this beginning the congregation grew and met in the freight room of the Parsons Depot. Then it met in the Masonic Hall until a frame building was constructed in 1893 at 213 Tennessee Avenue by Ike Buckner. The first organists were Miss Nettie Winston, Mrs. Kirk Jennings, Ada Medearis, Exie Houston, and Nellie Carrington.

As the congregation grew, a larger building was constructed in 1919 at the present location, 319 Tennessee Avenue South. Before the sanctuary was completed, members worshiped in the basement. C. S. Thomas was the pastor. Under the pastorate of Archie L. Partain, an educational building was added in 1952. Despite the addition more room was needed. In April of 1971, the pastor, Paul Shell, launched a building fund campaign to raise an estimated $225,000 for a new sanctuary. This dream became a reality on Easter Sunday in 1972.

Paul Shell remained at Parsons First Baptist Church as pastor from 1967 until 1974. Other pastors who have served this church were R. A. Kimbro, J. J. Ammerson, B. F. Parlow, N. B. Williams, A. U. Nunnery, J. A. Carmack, Frank Boren, Fleetwood Ball, Floyd Crittendon, E. K. Chapman, O. H. Huckabee, C. S. Thomas, T. M. Boyd, R. L. Bell, I. N. Penich, Joe Jennings, C. F. Lowery, L. P. Flemming, Roy Keathley, G. G. Joyner, T. T. Newton, W. R. Belew, H. L. Waters, Joe Cruse, D. Wade Smith, R. K. Bennett, D. Wade Carver, Archie Partain, Floyd Olive, Bill Hammonds, James A. Overton, and Allen Carter, who is presently serving.

First Baptist Church, Decaturville

On September 11, 1901, a group of people met for the organization of a Missionary Baptist Church in Decaturville. The first financial gift toward the establishment of a church building was recorded in February, 1901. A name seen often in the list of contributions was that of Mr. and Mrs. Curry P. Dennison. It is said that Mrs. Dennison and her untiring efforts were greatly responsible for the church building. A lot was purchased from the late Joe Jennings, a county official living in Decaturville at that time, who later became pastor of the new church. The entries on September 28, and October 4, show that $50 was paid each time for church pews. Elston Tate, about 21 at the time, was contractor and the elevated floor was something to see and talk about. The church was a one-story white frame building, 30 x 50 feet, with a two-door entrance.

At the first service in the building, T. F. Moore served as moderator for the group, and N. B. Williams was clerk. Those who came into the membership of the church on that day were Mr. and Mrs. C. P. Yarbro, Ora Yarbro, Ella Lacy, Allie Dennison, Joe H. Jennings, W. R. Dennison, and W. P. Maury. Maury was elected deacon and Jennings was elected church clerk;

Jennings and G. L. Dennison were elected delegates to the Beech River Baptist Association for that year.

Preaching in the early days of the church was usually one Sunday morning and evening service each month. One entry shows that the pastor was to receive $60.00 a year. The first Sunday School was started in 1912. Records also show that members were excluded or fellowship withdrawn for contempt of the church and heresy.

On March 16, 1947, the church voted unanimously to buy the lot in back of the church on which to construct a new building. Trustees appointed to transact this legal business were J. W. Tolley, Roy N. McPeak, Frank Scott, E. H. Wylie, and C. R. Avery. On April 23, 1947, the church voted to set up a building fund. The new building was completed in November of 1954. In 1966 during the pastorate of the late George Daigle, an educational building was added to the back of the auditorium.

Pastors to serve this church from its beginning in 1901 until 1954 were T. F. Moore, L. N. Pankey, E. Z. Newsome, A. L. Bray, G. S. Price, R. E. Guy, J. W. Barnett, Fleetwood Ball, A. U. Nunnery, W. L. King, Joe Jennings, J. Y. Butler, J. T. Bradfield, J. S. Bell, Earl Vaughn, L. F. Gassaway, A. M. Senter, C. B. Pennington, Woodward Bartholomew, R. K. Bennett, T. L. Maddux, and E. H. McCaleb. Pastors serving the church since 1954 were Reverend McCaleb, James F. Rogers, Grady Dozier, Edsel Pippens, Shelton Smith, George Daigle, James Smith, Don Evans, and Bill H. Smith. At present, David Miller, of Lexington, is serving as interim pastor.

Beacon Baptist Church

The Beacon Baptist Church was organized through the efforts of Wade Carver, pastor of Parsons First Baptist Church, after he led a successful effort in 1949 to buy a building, formerly owned by the Presbyterian Church, for a sanctuary. On May 25, 1950, a

council of members from Parsons First Baptist Church met in
Beacon. The council was composed of Reverend Wade Carver,
Reverend and Mrs. Millard Evans, Reverend C. R. Story, Nannie
Barnett, Lena Evans, Blanche Dodson, Ruth Evelyn Townsend,
and Ella Tranum. There were seven charter members: Erby
Sullivan, Maud Todd, Lillie Mae Harris, Lucille Dennison,
Valada Wise, Amealie Wallace and Dorothy Wallace. Through the
efforts of the Baptist Association in Nashville, Parsons First
Baptist Church, and the work of the members, the building that
had been bought was improved.

Reverend Millard Evans was succeeded by Reverend C. R.
Story. J. T. Todd served the church five years. Other pastors were
Darain Horn, Elmus Flowers, Tommy Harrell, Don Garrison,
Doug Sanders, David Walker, and Donald Bain. The present
pastor is Charley Broadway.

Corinth Methodist Church

The Methodist churches in Decatur County were in the
Decaturville Circuit, the Jackson District, and the Memphis
Conference. The 1885 report shows that there were eight
churches organized in this Circuit and four local preachers
served them. At the time there were 755 members total in the
eight congregations. One of the earliest of these churches was
Corinth Methodist.

Located between Scotts Hill and Saltillo, the Corinth
Methodist Church dates as far back as the early 1830s. It first
came into existence after Mary Dougherty Creasy with her four
sons, Stephen, John, Jeremiah, Ambros Ranson, and two daughters, Judy and Polly, traveled in a covered wagon from Goose
Creek, Virginia, to Decatur County about the year 1830. They
were believed to be the first settlers in the Thurman Community;
therefore, it is believed that they founded the Corinth Church.

There have been five different church structures and four
building sites since its founding. The first church structure was
located between Thurman and the Point Pleasant Road.

In 1968 the fifth Corinth church was erected to replace a frame one. It was constructed of concrete blocks with hardwood floors and electric heat. The walls were paneled. At the entrance of the church there was a foyer which had a Sunday School room on each side. A major portion of the construction was done by the people of the community, especially Reverend Neal Hinson, who donated all his time to lay all the concrete block structure.

Most of the families that attend Corinth are direct descendents of the first settlers of the Thurman Community. Some of these families that give their time and effort to help keep Corinth Church strong are Pafford Thomison and her children, Genie Mapul Wyatt, Oneava Mitchell, Faye McBride, the Tommy Wyatt family, Betty Kincannon Montgomery and family, Maggie Kincannon, the Gilbert Wyatt family, and the Charles D. Creasy family.

Mt. Nebo Methodist Church

Mt. Nebo Church building was erected shortly after Decatur became a county in 1845. It stemmed from a brush arbor revival held by a circuit rider. The first church was about 30 feet x 16 feet and constructed from hewn yellow poplar logs.

In 1885 the log building was torn down and a boxed church building erected. In 1908 the church was remodeled. The building was again renovated around 1955 and modernized with hardwood floors, gas heat, comfortable pews, and a beautiful altar. However, misfortune hit the little church on March 1, 1976, when it was destroyed by fire. A new brick structure was erected and the congregation moved into it in September of 1976.

Among early pastors of the church were Clovis Chappell, O. H. Lafferty, A. G. Barnes, W. E. Gibson, B. I. Crowder, who served from 1947-1952, Roy D. Williams, 1932, C. V. Stacks, 1933 and again in 1952, O. W. Brinkley, 1954-1955, John Archer, J. C. Agnew, 1958, B. D. Hooper, 1959, Phillip McClure, 1960, Robert Saywell, 1961, John Van Middleworth, John Churchwell,

1962, and Charlie White, 1967-1972. Other pastors were E. G. Gowan, L. A. Cruise, W. C. Baker, J. T. Banks, Tom Jones, and J. J. Maynard. The present pastor is Neil Hinson.

First Methodist Church, Decaturville

The first Methodist church in Decaturville was built in 1854. The first trustees were L. B. Stanfield, Lewis Garrett, S. Singleton, Henry Singleton, and Joseph Kelley. Within the church's history, it has had four different locations, three of which have been traced. The second one was on a lot purchased on November 29, 1871, from the Sons of Temperance, across the street from the present location. The building was a two-story frame structure housing the church on the ground level and the Masonic Lodge on the upper level. The church trustees negotiating this purchase were W. H. Johnson, D. M. Scott, O. P. Trem, D. M. Funderburk, and J. M. Porterfield. The pastor at this time was W. D. Stayton.

In 1910 the congregation moved to a new building located on a lot purchased from Decatur County Bank on June 18, 1909, on the west of the court square. Decatur County Farm Bureau building is now located on the site. It was a frame structure with intricate designs. Trustees involved in this transaction were W. Stout, J. T. Rogers, J. H. Evans, J. A. Culp, and G. E. Smith. W. D. Simmons was pastor. The frame building served the congregation until 1955, when a new brick building was built one block north of court square near the U. S. Post Office. To date, 54 ministers have served this church, the late O. H. Lafferty serving the longest period of time. The last addition to the church property occurred in 1970. Judge J. A. England and J. S. England, father and son, served as Sunday School superintendents for more than 60 years. Nina McMillan served the church over 68 years as organist and pianist, and J. W. Blount served as secretary and treasurer for 40 years.

Pleasant Hill United Methodist Church

Pleasant Hill United Methodist Church held services in a tent until 1926 when Jess Tucker led the building program to erect a church building. Replacing the small frame strucure in 1946 was a larger modern concrete block building.

The Pleasant Hill church is one of the four churches on the Bath Springs Circuit. Other churches are Keeton Springs, Mt. Nebo, and Center. The first pastor on the circuit was A. G. Barnes. Others who have served the circuit were Reverend Owens, F. A. Flatt, Guy Arant, James Bagby, William Scruggs, T. W. Steadman, Reverend Davis, Humbert Weir, C. B. Allen, John Archer, and Charles Brinkley. Serving as pastor in 1929 was J. P. Troutt of Sharon, and B. J. Crowder served from 1945 until 1948. From 1956 the following pastors have served the charge: Benny Hopper, Phillip McClure, David Haley, Charley White, and Neal Hinson. The present pastor is George Barnes.

Concord United Methodist Church

Ruben White, in consideration of his desire to promote the Methodist Episcopal Church South, especially at Concord, deeded to trustees Henry Welch, Curry Pettigrew, George W. Smith, John Coats, Nicholas D. White, David M. Scott, and George W. Harrel two acres of land on which a church house was to be erected. He also guaranteed the right to have passageway to a spring on his land about two hundred yards from the site. The deed was executed on August 7, 1869.

A log building was erected first which served as a temporary place of worship. The present building was constructed of native yellow poplar and was a one-room building 30 x 40 feet. Additions and improvements to this structure have been made in 1953, 1961, 1964, and 1973.

The first three preachers were W. D. Strayton, R. R. Nelson, and William Hay. Other preachers have been O. H. Lafferty, Dr. F. A. Hall, W. F. Cooley, and W. M. Vaughn. The present pastor is James W. Cotham.

Suttles United Methodist Church

Suttles Methodist Church was organized on January 8, 1897, according to a deed from W. L. Jernegan and wife. No earlier deed is available; however, old settlers think that the land was once owned by William P. Suttles, for whom the church received its name.

The first church was a one-room log building with hewn log seats. This building burned and was replaced by a small boxed building, which served until it was torn down for a larger building. On August 8, 1976, the foundation was laid for a new building since the old one was beyond repair.

I. S. Atkisson served as pastor during the new building program, at which time services were held in the home of Mr. and Mrs. John Newsom. At this time, women sat on one side of the church and men on the other side. Reverend Atkisson served the church for about 18 years. In 1909-1910, the enrollment was 23 male members and 29 females.

Salaries for the pastors in the early days were quite small. In 1913 Reverend Atkisson received $7.50 for the year. In 1910 the pastor received $8.55 a year, and in 1915 it increased to $28. By 1928 the salary reached $34 a year.

United Methodist Church, Parsons

Parsons United Methodist Church grew from services held in the first school building in Parsons located at 413 Tennessee Avenue South. The first church building was constructed in the early 1890s. It was located across the street from the present building at 109 East Third Street and was completed in the fall of 1893, according to an account in the *Messenger Newspaper,* edited by G. S. Barry. Henry Myracle donated the land for the church. Among the charter members were Mrs. W. G. Rains, Will Warden, Laverne Warden, Sam Warden, Tennie V. Arnold, Ada Pettigrew, Fannie Partin, Minnie Rains, Ethel Houston, Lizzie Terry, and Maggie Warden.

Economic conditions improved to the extent that in 1920 a brick building located directly across the street from the former one was constructed. Built by L. H. Nail, it was noted for its beautiful windows. Misfortune fell in December of 1957 when fire destroyed the building. Services were held at the Parsons Elementary School until February 1, 1959, when the new church building was completed. Marbury Hall, a larger educational building, was added in 1960. This addition was dedicated to Reverend Pittman Marbury who served the church from 1959 to 1961.

Northern Methodist Church, Parsons

The Northern Methodist Church in Parsons was located at the intersection of Florida Avenue and Third Street. It was constructed in 1893, a short time later than the Methodist Episcopal Church, South, now known as the United Methodist.

The church was a frame building and served the town until the two Methodist churches united. Clyda Lollar Boose was the last pastor to serve the church, having served in 1938 and 1939. She finished her high school education in Parsons and was the first woman ever ordained by the conference. After the unification of the northern and southern churches, she continued serving churches. She was ordained an elder at the First United Methodist Church in Memphis in 1946. Other pastors who served the Northern Methodist Church were Walter Phillips and Frank Blankenship.

Keeton Springs United Methodist Church

The first church building was on a hill and served as church and school combination. A second building was built in a valley below the hill. Robert "Bob" Keeton deeded the land for the church on January 1, 1900. A fine spring of cold water, known as the Clardy family spring, was nearby. The Keetons bought this farm from the Clardy family in 1851. In 1946 the second building was torn down, and services were held in the Union Hall school house until the new building was completed in 1948.

Among some of the older members are B. B. Keeton, Ora Keeton, John Keeton, Hester Keeton Brigance, Ben Brasher, Hester Brasher, Oval Keeton, Flora Keeton, Sarah Emily Keeton Adkisson, Robert F. Keeton, Lonie Lafferty, Gabe Tucker, Lena Artis, Omer Butler, Violet Butler, O. C. Cordle, Floyd Johnson, and Maynard Johnson.

St. Mark A.M.E. Church

The St. Mark A.M.E. Church originated in 1908 at the community known as Two-Foot in Parsons. Its frame structure served the black congregation until 1965 when a new brick building was erected. Located at 498 East Eighth Street in Parsons, the church has a membership of 38.

Built for approximately $10,000, the building includes a large sanctuary, two classrooms, and two bathrooms. It is finished on the inside with paneling and oak woodwork. The corner stone was laid in ceremonies on November 24, 1965, hosted by the Parsons Masonic Lodge No. 47, with Worshipful Master Roy Anders in charge. The presiding Bishop C. A. Gibbs of the 13th Episcopal District spoke at the three o'clock service.

Willie W. Wortham of Jackson was serving as the church's pastor during the building of the new church. He served at Freeman Chapel A.M.E. Church in Decaturville prior to serving the Parsons Church. He also assisted in the construction of a new brick church in Parsons in 1964 by a 42-member congregation.

Camp Ground Cumberland Presbyterian Church

If the Presbyterian churches are not the largest in the county, they do have the distinction of being some of the oldest. Between the years 1840-1845, during a religious era, the people of what is now Decatur County began to congregate and camp together for the purpose of worship. From this beginning, Camp Ground Cumberland Presbyterian Church was born. The land was donated by Gill Rushing, and a log church soon was built. It was constructed by 28 members in 1847. Located on the Decaturville and Beacon Road, this building was used for over 100 years of worship. It had great meaning for those in the community as well as those who moved away and returned on Decoration Day.

In 1953 a brick building was erected near the old log church. Later, after being used as a recreation center for a few years, the original church was torn down. The new building was dedicated by Reverend H. C. Watson of Jackson, Tennessee, with an all day service and dinner on the ground. J. J. Douglas was serving the church as pastor at this time. Through the years the church has never had a large membership, but it still has members whose ancestors were among early founders.

In the minutes dated March 4, 1870, Reverend John H. Day, Reverend T. C. Bell, and J. O. Lewis held a revival at the church. In 1879 J. W. Fitzgerald was serving the church as pastor. Elders serving at this time were Lawson Roberts, J. D. Rushing, and B. W. Myracle. Presently serving as elders of the church are Alvin Myracle, Elco Teague, Lewis Welch, and Fred Brasher. George Brasher is serving as Sunday School superintendent, Helen Welch Brasher is serving as church treasurer, and the pastor is David Lancaster.

Wesson Chapel Cumberland Presbyterian Church

Located in Sugar Tree, Wesson Chapel Cumberland Presbyterian Church dates back to 1896 and is named in honor of

Captain Nathaniel A. Wesson, a Decatur Countian who fought with the Confederate Army in the Civil War. Captain Wesson and his wife, Sarah, set aside land for the church as well as the Wesson Cemetery located on the opposite side of Sugar Tree.

Serving as pastors of the church have been W. T. Massey, 1897-1899; J. G. Anderson, 1899-1900; G. W. Crutches, 1900-1901; J. G. Anderson, 1902-1913; W. C. Sanders, 1913-1914; John McIllwain, 1914-1922; T. H. Sundarth, 1922-1929; George McIllwain, 1932-1937; W. D. Marlar, 1937-1941; J. J. Douglas, 1941-1944; Sam Nail, 1944-1948; John Ellis, 1949-1950; George McIllwain, 1950-1952; Clinton Buck, 1952-1955; Hillman Moore, 1955-1957; Don McConnell, 1957-1959; Tommy Conblee, 1960-1961; Cardell Smith, 1962-1968; Don Laruee, 1969-1971; Tommy Walker, 1971-1972; Raymond Boroughs, 1973-1975. Jimmy Messer is the present pastor.

Early members of the church were Sarah Wesson, T. C. Robertson, Robert Robertson, Will Robertson, S. C. Robertson, J. F. Farlow, J. K. Pagnew, S. J. Wesson, Joe Odle, C. W. Odle, H. L. Odle, D. R. Odle, M. B. Fisher, W. G. Fry, Mrs. D. R. Odle, Mrs. M. B. Fisher, W. G. Fry, Viola Odle, Flora Odle, Mrs . Willie Odle, Lillian Walker, Nattie Fisher, and Sadie Farlow Robertson, all who joined in 1897. Other early members include J. J. Odle, R. W. Wesson, Joe Wesson, Mollie W. Farlow, Mrs. Herkie Thomas, Lucy Odle, Emma Odle Townsend, Maude Odle, Bess Odle, R. T. Wesson, Suzanna Bray, Dora Walker Wesson, S. J. Wesson, B. H. Maxwell, and wife, Alice Maxwell.

Cumberland Presbyterian Church, Beacon

The Cumberland Presbyterian Church at Beacon was organized by an A. M. C. Gossett in 1893. Services were held in the school building prior to the construction of a new church. The foundation was laid for the church building in September of 1893. The land was deeded by Kit Thomas. Elders of this church in the 1930s were C. R. Matlock, Thades Hayes, Murray Norman, and Troy Alexander. Jessie Douglas served as pastor in the early

1930s. The membership at that time was around 25 and declining. For this reason the church membership moved to Parsons. In 1948 the First Cumberland Presbyterian Church was built in Parsons on Virginia Avenue. Members from Beacon assisted in its construction.

Cumberland Presbyterian Church, Parsons

Reverend J. E. Flemming, field man for the Synod of West Tennessee, visited Parsons and contacted a number of people who expressed interest in having a Cumberland Presbyterian church there. Also I. M. Vaughn, clerk of the Madison Presbytery, made several visits to Parsons in 1946-1947, giving encouragement to the efforts of the people.

On April 28, 1947, a number of interested persons met at the Farmers Bank in Parsons and appointed a local committee on building and finance. The committee was composed of B. C. Dailey, chairman, Vernal Pettigrew, C. B. Livingston, Dean Livingston, Edith Marchbanks, Erlby Mae Marshbanks, Reverend J. J. Douglas, and R. C. Livingston. At a meeting of the Madison Presbytery, October 14, 1947, in Lexington, Tennessee, a commission composed of B. L. Rochelle, O. J. Douglas, and I. M. Vaughn was appointed to raise funds and to construct a building in Parsons.

On October 31, 1948, Reverend J. T. Buck and Reverend and Mrs. Vaughn Fults began a revival in the new building. The attendance at the first service was 80. The revival closed with 51 persons enrolled as charter members. The people gave $165 to cover incidental expenses of the revival and presented Reverend and Mrs. Fults with an offering of $200 as an expression of appreciation.

The charter membership included R. C. Livingston, Martha Livingston, Lester Marchbanks, Byrda M. Pratt, Lillian Walker, Exie Bowman, Mr. and Mrs. Charlie Kindle, Mr. and Mrs. C. S. Livingston, Mrs. A. J. Dailey, Mrs. Wesley Dailey, H. L. Riley, Roxie Miller, Bonnie M. Hayes, Annie Riley, Peggy Riley, Mrs. J. J. Odle, Rebecca McIllwain, Claudie Hooten, O. J. Douglas, J. H.

Hays, Mr. and Mrs. J. W. P. Lewis, Opal Douglas, Doris Douglas, Thelma Douglas, Mr. and Mrs. Jack Goff, Lela McMurry, Ida Lackey, Lena Yates, Nell Farlow, Lorna Hooton Cotham, Dorothy Greer, Bertha Taylor, W. E. Lackey, Everett McIllwain, Mrs. J. L. Cotham, Mrs. J. J. Spence, Harold Logan Spence, Vernal W. Pettigrew, Inez Davis Pettigrew, Mr. and Mrs. W. A. Tuck, Collins Wesson, Dean Livingston, Lawana Bohannon, and Sue McMurray. The first pastor to serve the new church was Marion L. Garrett. He was followed by Morris Clerk. Others who have served are J. Howard Scott, Vernon Burrow, Sam Wayman, J. W. Dancer, Julian Welch, Marvin Wilkins, Kermit E. Neal, Harold Reeves, and the present pastor, Bill Herringlake.

Church of Christ

Around 1908 a few people who had heard the gospel proclaimed by ministers of the Church of Christ decided to start a congregation in Decatur County. Those instrumental in the initial movement were Frank Alexander, Jim Myracle, John "Doc" Myracle, Bill Elliott, Tom Smalls, Frank Hays, Ike Hayes, B. Hayes, W. F. Bowman, G. W. Haggard, Jeff Steed, and Milt Houston.

Frank Alexander agreed to give the land, as well as timber from his farm, on which to build a meetinghouse. Volunteers rallied and Bill Elliott also gave timber. The building was destroyed later by high winds. These valiant men quickly went into action, and another building was erected. Ironically, this building also was destroyed by high winds. It was located in the heart of Beacon, on the Beacon-Decaturville Road.

From this discouraging beginning, brethren from Beacon and Parsons got together to construct a meetinghouse about halfway between their towns. Henry Hendrix gave the land, and the building was erected on the hill west of Johnson's Creek and called Center Hill. This place served the congregation for a time. Later the Parsons group began meeting in the city's abandoned Northern Methodist Church. In the 1950s, the Parsons congregation built a church on Tennessee Avenue South. Instrumental in the erection of the building were Herman Rains, John Frank Alexander, and George Jordan. The Beacon Congregation met in the schoolhouse until they built a one-room small block building which still serves them.

Early members were Will Neely, Arthur Baugus, Will Jordan, J. C. Duck, Betty Baugus, and Lena Jordan. Pastors who have served the church are Willie Bradfield, Brother Luckett, Joe Williams, Brother Pogue, Bill Johnson, Lester Coats, Bobby Pinkley, Guy Hester, Joe Cook Vandyke, and James Hinkle. The present pastor is Earl Cook. Serving as elders are George Jordan, John Frank Alexander, Lewis Welch, and Bob Adams. Deacons include Jerry Bell, Gary Hall, Obie Hendrix, Larry Lindsey, Larry Parrish, Harold Seagraves, Roscoe Stegall, and Larry Tyler.

Saul Paul Church of Christ

The Saul Paul Church of Christ was located two miles south of Hog Creek. The building was constructed of poplar lumber and had one big room that served for Sunday School and preaching services. The building was destroyed by a storm in 1920 and was never rebuilt.

Among the early members were Eason Frazier, George Spence, Bob Spencer, Jim Faulkner, Dick and William Cotham, Paul S. Spencer, Carrie Baker, and Marvin Spencer.

Another early Church of Christ was located one-half mile south of Jeanette. It was a one-story building constructed in the 1890s. Among the church leaders were Will Jordan, Arthur Baugus, Maggie Baugus, Mrs. Johnnie Spencer, and Betty Cotham Baugus. The church declined, and members went to surrounding churches in the early 1900s.

Central Church of Christ, Decaturville

Central Church of Christ was established by Mr. and Mrs. Eldridge Stricklin, Bonnie Davis, Mr. and Mrs. Teddy Myracle, Betty Baugus, Mr. and Mrs. Max Townsend, Jerry and Marilyn Townsend, Opal Kelley, Dennis Evans, Lela Hayes, Carolyn Patterson, Timmy, Jimmy, and Dwight Patterson, Mrs. Paul Goodman, Paula and Jana Goodman, Mr. and Mrs. Eddie Alvey and son, and Mrs. Freddie Brasher and children in April of 1969. Services, first held in an old service station building at the corner of Highways 69 and 100 in Decaturville, were moved later to the American Legion Building. A milestone was reached January 18, 1970, when the members of the church moved into their new $35,000 brick structure located in the northern edge of Decaturville.

Ministers working with the church from its institution were Eddie Alvey, Elgin Howard, Bob Prater, Richard England, and Tom Scott. Cliff Bennett and Gary McDade are presently serving the church as minister and associate minister. In the summer of 1973, the Decaturville Church of Christ united with the Central Church of Christ.

First United Pentecostal Church, Parsons

In the early part of 1944, three Pentecostal ministers, living in the town of Parsons and knowing of several persons of this faith who were making their homes in or near town, felt the need for a place of worship. After much consideration, these men planned a revival during that year. Reverend E. J. Douglas, Reverend A. N. Graves, and Reverend W. M. McClure contacted Reverend A. D. Gurley of Corinth, Mississippi, who began a revival campaign in September of 1944.

At the close of the two weeks revival, on Sunday, September 24, 1944, Reverend Gurley, who was also district superintendent of the Pentecostal Church, Incorporated, organized the Parsons Pentecostal Church with 25 members. The congregation elected

W. M. McClure as the first pastor of this new church. Plans were begun at once for a church building, and on the day the church was organized, some $1800 was raised in pledges and cash. Weekly services were held in homes while the committee was in the process of finding a building site. On May 1, 1945, a small house was rented for worship services, and the Parsons Pentecostal Sunday School was organized.

With the building committee and pastor working hard, a building site was purchased in the 800 block of Tennessee Avenue South, and a basement building was soon completed for worship services. The first service was conducted in this building on November 17, 1945, with Reverend Rexie Wilcox of Memphis as the main speaker. During the pastorate of Reverend R. B. Boyd, the main structure of the church was erected, being completed in 1955. The building committee consisted of Reverend Boyd, Russell Graves, Osco Taylor, Jim Camper, C. L. Yates, and Reverend A. N. Graves.

Mt. Tabor Pentecostal Church

The Mt. Tabor Pentecostal Church, located on the Old Decaturville Road near Parsons, has roots deep in Decatur County's history. Not far from the present church location once stood a log structure that was built in 1840. This building was used as both a school and a church. A Methodist congregation worshipped there and was pastored by a "circuit rider."

A revival was held near the log building in 1918. The evangelist was Reverend E. J. Douglas, one of the first Pentecostal ministers to have visited the area. Services were usually held outdoors under a "brush arbor," but when inclement weather came, they were conducted in the old log school and church. At the close of the revival, Walter and Francis Herndon, Jim and Bertha Graves, and Will and Ethel Graves signed a deed donating property for a new church. A building was started immediately and is still in use today.

The founding pastor was E. J. Douglas. The first trustees were A. D. Gurley (later to become one of the most renowned evangelists and respected ministers in the United Pentecostal Church International), Walter Herndon, and J. A. Graves. Others attending the new church were Antha Graves, Georgie Graves, Ruby Graves, Otis Graves, Carrie Gurley, Clyde Gurley, Grady Gurley, Mittie Herndon, Ester Houston, Mollie Lancaster, Eliza McIllwain, and Antha Stone.

Other Pentecostal Churches in Decatur County include Mt. Carmel United Pentecostal Church, Beacon United Pentecostal Church, Decaturville Pentecostal Church, Rushings Grove Pentecostal Church, Iron Hill Pentecostal Church, Full Gospel Pentecostal Church, and Sulphur Springs Pentecostal Church. The United Pentecostal churches have played an important part in the religious life of persons in Decatur County. In April of 1949 a resolution to make the Southern District, consisting of the states of Alabama, Mississippi, and Tennessee, three separate districts was passed. W. M. Greer of Jackson was elected to serve as the superintendent of the Tennessee District.

In 1950 the first plot of ground was purchased on "Holiness Hill" in Perryville for a campground site from E. O. Reed and wife of Madison County. After the district conference at Nashville in April of 1951, the sound of the hammers and saws was soon heard as the construction of rustic buildings that were to serve as a dining hall and tabernacle began. J. W. Wallace served as builder. Soon a number of cabins were also erected, lights came to the "Hill," and in August of 1951 the district started what was thought to be only a token campmeeting that turned out to be a history making event with hundreds in attendance.

In 1972, a vision was fulfilled with the erection of a home and office building for the district which became a center for the promotion, planning, and administering of the many functions of a growing organization. The campground continued to expand with the acquisition of more land and more buildings being erected.

Reverend A. N. Graves was instrumental in getting this camp underway. He played an important part, not only in the building, but in supervising of maintenance afterwards. From Memphis to Kingsport throughout the years, people have attended the camp meeting.

In 1954, Reverend W. M. Greer and the district board organized the Ladies Auxiliary who appointed Lela Holland president, and Mrs. Benthal Crossnoe as secretary. In 1958, Nana Benson was appointed as president and Doris Moore as secretary. In 1951 Tennessee board members included J. H. Austin, J. O. Moore, E. J. Douglas, W. M. Greer, D. B. Williams, R. G. Jackson, J. W. Wallace, E. E. McNatt, and W. T. Scott.

Reverend W. M. Greer is still serving as superintendent of the Tennessee District.

Trinity Tabernacle Assembly of God Church

Trinity Tabernacle Assembly of God Church is labeled a twentieth century miracle by the founder, Reverend Ralph Duncan. He and his wife Diane moved to Decaturville December 13, 1967, to launch a crusade. From this beginning, this couple felt led to remain in the county seat town. The congregation first met in various buildings until the new church was constructed.

In March of 1968, the congregation borrowed money to erect the edifice. On August 31, 1968, the pastor made the final payment at the bank. The first Sunday in September the property note was burned, and the attendance had reached 50. Construction began in January of 1969. The congregation continued to grow rapidly, and by the grand opening day August 1, 1969, the building was already inadequate. Two classrooms were added. In 1973 excavation began for a building to tie into the first structure making the floor space in both structures 20,000 square feet and bringing the total cost to approximately a quarter of a million dollars.

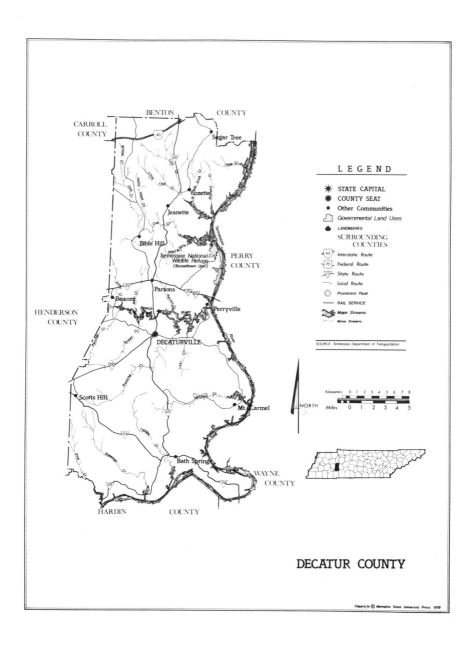

LEGEND

✳ STATE CAPITAL
◉ COUNTY SEAT
• Other Communities
⬠ Governmental Land Uses
⬟ LANDMARKS
SURROUNDING
       COUNTIES
🛈40 Interstate Route
🛈70 Federal Route
🛈13 State Route
Local Route
☼ Prominent Peak
RAIL SERVICE
Major Streams
Minor Streams

SOURCE Tennessee Department of Transportation

Kilometers 0 1 2 3 4 5 6 7 8
Miles 0 1 2 3 4 5

NORTH

DECATUR COUNTY

Roads and Transportation

Thousands of years ago huge animals roamed this country. Great herds wandered from pastures to watering places, and from salt licks to meadows. Later, buffalo were the largest animals that traveled similar paths; and in time, Indian trails frequently followed the paths of these animals. Today, even after hundreds of years, sometimes one may find a strip of sunken path resembling the old Indian trails. Traders, hunters, and settlers tended to follow Indian trails that crossed mountains into Tennessee country. Later, frontier days found stage coaches cutting more trails through the country on what were then called "stage roads."

The first stage line through the southern end of Decatur County began following buffalo trails in Carrolville, a small river landing town located on Clifton Bend of the Tennessee River. The route included the Cade's place and continued by Lone Chestnut to Dr. Hancock's place, located near the center of Bath Springs. Then it passed by the Shannon place just off Highway 114, went in front of Red House stage stop, and on to the Stevens and McCorkle places. There it ascended a steep hill, called "McCorkle Hill," and then continued to Dunbar. The route crossed the present Highway 100 at Browns Crossing into Scotts Hill and Cane Creek near Sugar Hill, then continued on to Lexington. From Lexington the stage line went to Jackson via Wolf Ridge, a very lonely and desolate road to travel. After the Civil War, a segment of the road was developed from Bob's Landing, formerly known as Shannonville.

An early road in the northern end of the county near Henderson County was known as the "Bucksnort Road." This road was an outlet for Perryville, which was a favorite shipping point for water transportation in early days. This road wound around Pikes Peak Springs and through Hopewell Community near the present site of the fire tower. It then crossed Cub Creek, except when a rain forced area travel through Jeanette, formerly known as Howesville.

Before the day of the turnpikes, a gravel road linked Parsons and Decaturville. A part of this road is still in use from Parsons to Riverside High School. It took a westward course at the present Riverside High School and crossed Beech River over a bridge that was constructed of stone pillows, steel frame and railings, and wooden floor. Traffic crossing the floor's wooden planks made a tremendous noise. Buckner Mill was located near the bridge. After crossing the bridge south toward Decaturville, traffic had to ascend a steep winding hill, known as Buckner's Hill. In early days it was a rare T-Model Ford that could pull the hill in high gear. The bridge was replaced and named the Arthur Tolley Bridge honoring the late funeral director. The road continued to Decaturville Foodland where it crossed the highway and entered Decaturville by what is presently known as the old Decaturville Road, passing by the homes of Guy Butler, E. C. Kennedy, and Boss Thompson. It rejoined the highway at the Baptist Church near F & P Food market. The old Perryville Road left Parsons at Second Street East, in front of the present Parsons Post Office. It wound its course by the Parsons Cemetery, over rocks and rills and around numerous curves to come out at Perryville by the Baptist Church. An old landmark on this road is known as the Old Townsend Place, now occupied by Mrs. David Yarbro. This road is still in use despite the fact a new highway runs parallel with it.

As population and business grew, so did the need for more and better roads. In 1804 the legislature gave permission to construct roads, bridges, and ferries. The expense of construction and upkeep was to be covered by small toll charges. This meant that counties had to furnish money needed for construction with the hope of repayment from toll money. The legislature set the toll charge to prevent turnpike companies from taking advantage of farmers and travelers.

The only county toll turnpike was known as the Decatur County Turnpike. It was organized in 1908 by Harry Burke, Hood Long, Dr. R. Y. Fisher, Wid Long, and E. M. Vise and was granted a charter by the General Assembly. These men financed construction of the five-mile stretch connecting Parsons and

Decaturville. The Dycus Brothers of Wayne County were low bidders and received the contract for construction. The road was built out of native phosphate boulders crushed by sledge hammers at a cost of $1000 a mile. A grader, pulled by four mules, and a mule-drawn scoop served as the main equipment. Walter, Jess, and Rube Hearington hauled the crushed phosphate. To finish the job, a huge roller also pulled by mules smoothed the gravel. The construction took about a year to complete.

The first toll gate was set up two miles from Parsons near Mount Tabor. Bill Woodard was the first toll keeper. The toll gate changed locations each time there was a new keeper. Toll was 25¢ for a wagon with a double team, 15¢ for a buggy and horse, and five cents for horseback riders, as well as cattle, horses, and hogs. For those fortunate enough to own a car, the toll charge was 25¢, with no extra charge for passengers.

The organizers of the toll turnpike lost money on the venture. The toll did not pay enough after the tenders were paid. In 1920 the county freed the road when it assumed road construction and maintenance. Today the road is no longer called a turnpike, but it is still one of the leading county thoroughfares being a link with Highway 100. This strip was widened and resurfaced in 1964 and a portion of it is a three-lane highway.

An event that played a major part in the economic growth of Decatur County was the building of the mile-long Alvin C. York Memorial Bridge across the Tennessee River at Perryville. The bridge generated a trucking industry for the towns of Parsons, Decaturville, and Linden in Perry County. Construction began in 1928, and the bridge was opened for traffic July 5, 1930. Built at a cost of two-thirds of a million dollars, it made the county much more accessible to traffic and commerce.

The bridge was first opened as a toll bridge with a fare of 50¢ per car and an additional five cents for each passenger, and one dollar for trucks. A coupon book was issued at a discount to trucks making regular trips. The toll bridge coupons were $2.50 per book. Coupons were for 12¢ and 13¢ each.

Alvin C. York Bridge across Tennessee River on opening day, July 5, 1930.

The largest income reported during the eight years that Dick Howard served as toll keeper was $300 in one day; however, business later increased. Others who served as toll keepers were Al Conder, Malcom Pratt, Tom Dees, Val Johnson, and Dick Hooten. The toll was discontinued February 4, 1947, with the introduction of a bill by the late Morg Conder.

The construction of a gravel road from Parsons to Lexington began in 1930. Later it was concreted in 1933 and 1934. A contract, dated May 31, 1930, was signed by W. A. Partin, Mayor Albert Bowman, L. F. Hufstedler, E. J. Houston, and H. R. Rains. The road was known as State Highway 20 and linked with Highway 100 in Parsons.

Today Decatur County is blessed with good roads. Highways include 20, 100, 114, and 69, the major highways, and numerous well-graveled roads throughout the county. Presently, U. S. Highway 641 is under construction. It crosses Decatur County in its trek through Henry, Benton, and Hardin counties from the northern to the southern border of Tennessee.

Long before construction of good roads in the county, the ferries at Perryville were the main form of transportation. They linked Perry and Decatur counties and played an important part in the settling of the county. Will Dennison owned what was known as the upper ferry, and James Walker Howard owned the lower ferry. These operated within 1000 yards of each other. As good roads emerged, the once thriving business began to dwindle.

Among those who operated ferries at Perryville were Henry Churchwell, Herbert (Preacher) Churchwell, and Clyde Young. Henry Churchwell served in this capacity until his death in 1925 at which time his son, Herbert, continued the operation. Clyde Young began as ferry operator in 1929 and continued until Alvin C. York Bridge accomodated the increasing traffic. Other ferries serving Decatur County in pioneer days were located at Point Pleasant, Bob's Landing, Vise Town Landing, and Clifton Landing which at present is still in operation.

Steamboats marked the dawn of a new day in commerce when they began to appear on the area rivers. Earlier transportation had been confined to self-powered rafts and flatboats, as well as skiffs and canoes.

Landings along the Tennessee River in Decatur County include Crew's Landing, which was located near the Benton County line; Parker's Landing where Jim Buck Warren ran a store in 1908; and Bohannon Landing where Scott Bohannon had a large warehouse and store; and Brodie's Landing which received its name from Charles S. Brodie, an early settler who owned 5000 acres of land there. Later Bohannon's warehouse and store belonged to B. M. Maxwell. Other county landings on the Tennessee River were Bateman Landing; Perryville Landing, one of the larger landings and one that is still in existence today; and Fisher's Landing, which was later owned by Jack Reynolds who had a big store. Up the river from Fisher's Landing were Martin's Landing and the Brownsport Landing, which came into existence in the 1860s to service the Brownsport Furnace.

Located five miles southwest of Bath Springs between Eagle Nest Island and Dickey Island is Swallow Bluff Landing. The

Steamboat "Clyde" at Perryville Landing, 1910.

three-fourth mile long bluff received its name during the Civil War when the swallows flew in the spring of 1862 and built nests from mud, stick, and straw under the huge layers of limestone rocks.

As the upward swing of the river course esculated, there were Garrett's Landing, Elkin's Landing, and Vise Landing, located below White's Creek. Here a big warehouse and store was operated by the Smith-Vise Company. W. G. Smith owned a cotton gin there in the early days. The picturesque site of Cedar Bluff Landing has been developed in recent years by Mr. and Mrs. J. T. Lafferty, and numerous homes have been constructed.

Double Island Landing, Martin's Landing, Point Pleasant, and Bob's Landing also played an important part in the early days of the county. Martin's Landing was located a short distance from

Bath Springs. Point Pleasant Landing was located in Clifton Bend.

The last landing in Decatur County was Bob's Landing. At one time, this thriving river landing was bustling with business. It was first named Shannonville for Bob Shannon, an early area settler. Later the name was changed to Bob's Landing due to difficulties in the postal service, since there was already a post office named Shannonville.

Railroads contributed greatly to the growth of Decatur County. The Tennessee Midland Railroad Company was chartered on December 29, 1886. It was to extend from Memphis eastwardly to the Virginia state line, ending in Hancock County near the Clinch River. Construction on the track from Memphis to Jackson began in 1887 and was completed by June 1, 1888. Construction then was started from Jackson to Perryville with 11.01 miles of track within the county.

R. H. Pentecost of Lexington was supervisor of the roadway, and Will Warden of Parsons served as buyer for lumber used to build the Perryville branch. Benjamin Franklin Streigel, originally from Merrill, Wisconsin, was the contractor of the trestle work and grading of fills. He supplied the piling for the trestles along with the necessary laborers and mules. The laborers were primarily Italian, German, and Irish, as well as local. Laborers who eventually settled in this vicinity were John Kneareen, Lew Seltzer, Patrick Fallan, and Walter Harris.

The track was completed to Perryville in 1889, but it was never extended beyond the Tennessee River due to lack of funding. The first train puffed into Perryville on June 30, 1889, loaded with passengers, mail, and freight. It consisted of six coaches—one coach for whites, one coach for blacks, one baggage car, and three freight cars. Among the train's first passengers were officials and construction and local workers.

The Perryville branch was responsible for a number of towns developing along its track in both Henderson and Decatur counties; some of these communities were Warren's Bluff, Chesterfield, Darden, Beacon, and Parsons.

Handcar and section crew, 1907. Citco service station is now where station stood. *Left to right seated front:* Captain Conger, Henry Clay; *left to right standing:* Jim Houston, Jess Houston, Elzie Conger, Bill Hayes, Wash Riggs, Charlie Clay, Ed McElrath.

Serving as depot agents on the line at Perryville were Will Andrews, Luther Hurst, George Peck, from Michigan, O. C. Kirksey, from Yuma, Tennessee, George O'Guinn, from Beacon, Tennessee, and John A. Tinker, from Decatur County. Parsons depot agents were John Young, B. F. Goodlow, H. L. (Crickett) Veal, W. H. Neely, Hubert Boren, and John A. Tinker, who served after the Perryville station was closed and moved to Parsons. Serving as depot agents at Beacon were Tip Oxford, Ebern Kirksey, Glen Batton, George O'Guinn, Dick Joyner, and Hobart Hayes. Later Jess Long served as caretaker. John Tinker served as depot agent in Perryville, until the railroad closed there. He then was transferred to Parsons to serve in the place of the ailing Hubert Boren.

The railroad began losing money with the advent of good highways in the county. On February 10, 1936, the L and N and the N. C. & St. L. railroads filed an application with the Interstate Commerce Commission for a certificate of public convenience and necessity to abandon operation of the Perryville branch, all in Henderson and Decatur counties.

The shrilling sound of the train whistle, the puffing of the engine while filling up with water at Parsons water tank, and the call of the conductor naming the towns on the once important Perryville Branch Line came to an end on October 31, 1936. The coaches were filled with citizens from the county on this day for a last ride on the "PeeVine."

Boat, cart, buggy, train, all were to give way to a form of transportation that was at once more phenomenal, more personal, more efficient, and faster, a vehicle that was to become the trademark of the United States—the automobile.

One of the first owners of an automobile in Decatur County was George Partin of Parsons. In 1912, Teddy Roosevelt gave him a six-cylinder, open type, used Ford for his services in the presidential campaign. The first car in Parsons, it was shipped from Chicago by flat railroad car.

Fred Rains drove the Partin Ford to Mt. Tabor where a brush arbor was used in a summer revival and broke up the service since it was the first car many had seen. The noise was deafening,

The curved trestle near Perryville and the Perryville branch train making its last run from Perryville to Lexington October 12, 1935.

and the congregation heard it long before it came in sight. Even the preacher said he had never seen a car, and he was going to see this one, so he stopped preaching to go out to see it.

The public transportation that Decatur County lost with the closing of the railroad has been replaced by airplanes. Parsons municipal airport, Scott Field, was built in 1959 at a cost of a quarter of a million dollars and was financed by state, county, and city funds with no federal aid. It was named for Madison Scott, mayor when the city acquired the airport and an avid flyer.

In 1964, a building was constructed on the ground with office space, lounge, lobby, and snack bar. With a runway 3000 feet long north and south, the airport is on a direct route from

Nashville to Memphis and is located in the industrial area of Parsons, adjoining the National Guard Armory on 9th Street.

People who fly here include businessmen, salesmen, sportsmen, politicians, and local enthusiasts. Private planes are housed there, and Parsons boasts the Parsons Flying Club. The airport has been very important to the six industries in Decatur County as well as to other surrounding industries.

Another early car in Parsons was a second-hand Studebaker owned by Leslie A. Rains. He traded a nice stallion for the Studebaker which was valued at $1200. Carl Partin purchased a new Chevrolet from McGee-Ross in Jackson in 1916.

In 1912, Ray McClanahan became the first car agent in Decatur County when he took the Ford agency at Scotts Hill. Other early dealers in Decatur County were Wylie Stout and Jim England who had the Ford agency in Decaturville. Hobart Goff was employed as a salesman. In 1923-1924 Hobart Goff and G. C. Pollard sold Durant cars and Star cars in Parsons. In the 1920s Herbert Roberts had the Chevrolet agency in Parsons. He later moved away and J. C. Partin became the dealer. Partin went out of business, and in 1935 Wilburn Townsend and Leonard Townsend opened up the present Chevrolet agency. It is presently operated by Wayne Townsend.

Jack Stevens had the Ford agency in Parsons in the early 1930s. In 1944, Hobart Goff opened a Ford dealership and operated it until his retirement. His sons, Billy and James Goff, then took over the dealership, and later James was sole operator. In 1966, James Goff went out of business and G. L. Teague and Dr. Paul Ford Teague became Ford agents in Parsons. In 1974, Roger Voiner joined the firm.

Will Long had the agency for the Brisco car at Perryville in the early 1900s and later came to Parsons and was dealer for the Studebaker in the 1930s, as well as Chryslers, Plymouths and International Trucks. In 1951, Doug Hayes took over the agency. Another early car dealer was Weaver Rogers who had the agency for the Kaiser-Frazier car. Poolie Bateman was also a car dealer in Parsons. He sold Overland cars in the early 1920s.

Decatur County Schools

Free schools opened in Decatur County in 1869 with J. W. Morgan serving as school superintendent. The scholastic population from six to 20 years of age was 1198 male whites and 1123 female whites with 159 male blacks and 301 female blacks. There were 34 civil district school directors in the county. They were D. L. Lancaster, J. J. Lancaster, N. Turnbo, E. M. Crain, Lewis Kindle, W. D. Wyatt, C. Roberts, S. K. Gill, Morris Veal, W. L. Louis, H. G. Woodard, M. M. Ward, D. C. Petty, J. C. Graves, W. S. Swafford, W. W. Liles, M. Joy, J. S. Bagby, S. J. Outery, Willie Smothers, H. S. Cagle, D. C. Kennedy, J. H. Fry, Green Munger, F. M. Morgan, George Morgan, A. Jones, William Holland, A. N. Allen, Stephen Creasey, S. W. Riggs, E. D. Bostic, T. W. McMurry, and Samuel Hancock.

Before free schools, the early schools organized in Decatur County, or what was to become Decatur County, were called academies. Often held in church buildings, these academies usually had one teacher who taught all grades—primer through the eighth. Because of the necessity for most students to work in the fields, school terms were short, running about three months through the winter and three through the summer when possible. One of the first of these schools was the Academy of Perryville built in 1821 of logs, with yellow poplar paneling and ceiling. Located in the center of the town, it was later made into a house and became the home of B. F. Striegle; however, the structure was torn down in the late 1950s.

Initially, schools dotted the rural areas. One of the first school buildings to be erected in the county was Mt. Tabor School. It was constructed of logs, a one-room building located two miles south of Parsons on the old Decaturville road, and was used as a church-school combination in pioneer days.

Among teachers who had taught at Mt. Tabor were Sam Duck, J. C. Duck, Naomi Jones, Lelia Conder, Mrs. Ray Bloodworth, Mrs. Pike Vise Johnson, Thelma Odle, Vesta Morris, Roy Duck, Eunice Gooch, and Cora Gooch.

Another school listed among the first in the county was in Decaturville. It was built on lot 99 which was purchased for an academy shortly after 1845. Called Decaturville Academy, it was located somewhere between the present Health Center and the cemetery. The trustees of the academy were J. L. Houston, J. A. Rains, H. C. Fryar, William Henry, and David R. Funderburk.

An early school also located in Decaturville was the Crowder School, named for the founder, Dave Crowder, an outstanding educator of his time. The school started as a one-year high school after grammar school. Then it became a two-year high school and later a three-year high school. After the death of the founder, the school became an elementary school, and the students ready for high school had to go to Montgomery High School in Lexington.

F. L. Black revived the school in 1946 and organized it eventually into an "A" rated four-year high school. After Black's death in 1953, S. F. Dobbins took over and the school lasted until the integration of schools in Decatur County in 1965 when Riverside High School consolidated the county high schools.

Among the early teachers at Crowder School, which was located a mile west of the court square, were Jim Crowder, Dave Crowder, Anna Crowder, Gretchen Craig, Clara Montgomery, S. F. Dobbins, Geneva Menzies, Novella Tole, Pauline Phelps, Henry Sanders, Porter Boyd, F. H. Duck, S. A. Crenshaw, Alvin Sharpe, Lorraine Mays, Lovie Lee Rogers, Velma Holt, Gertrude Sharp, Ethel Meeks, Mary Randolph, Jewel Strawn, and William Bates.

Mt. Nebo, located 15 miles south of Decaturville, was another pioneer school, having been established shortly after Decatur became a county. The log building was used for both school and church. Some of those who taught there prior to 1928 were Ernestine Tuten Keeton, Jessie Akin Fisher, Steve Eason, Ben Lentz, Guy Butler, Andy Steele, Bertie Dailey, Henry McKinney, and Eula Martin Rogers.

Another early school was Spence School, a church-school combination, located in the Spence Cumberland Presbyterian Church building. Later a new school building was erected. The land for the building was given by George Spence's family and thus it received its name from it. Located 12 miles north of Parsons, it was a one-room frame building as well as a one-teacher school, with grades from the primer through the eighth.

Some of the early teachers were Zoedie Cox Bell, Pearl Cox Tippet, Clifford Tubbs, Jack Moore, Ernest Higdon, Sallie Spence, and Mrs. Gray King. During Mrs. King's term a school picture was made. Listed in the picture were Patterson Allen, Loddie Allen, Ruby Allen Boyd, Ressie Douglas Stokes, Rosie Spence Haynes, Georgie Spence, Melton Ballinger, Connie Harris, Felix Spence, Helen Webb Hughs, Myrtle Sanders Hill, Wilford Spence, Lynn Bawcum, Eulan Cox, Walter Mederist, Albert Cantrell, George Cantrell, Lorene Cantrell, Willie Ballinger, Zelmer Douglas, Dewey Douglas, Hurman Frazier, Jim Spence, Leon Franks, Thelma Sanders Franks, Irene Franks Coble, Mable Franks Green, Ruth Franks Jordan, Hallie Webb Hughs, Willie Frazier Odle, Bessie Frazier McAuley, Ellen Spence Modlin, Beady Sanders Bawcum, Sallie Spence, and Mrs. Gray Ballinger King.

Lunsford School, located three and one-half miles east of Parsons between the Iron Hill and Hopewell communities, was also an early institution of learning. It was a one-room frame structure perhaps 20 x 30 feet and was used exclusively for a school.

The school term was convenient to the farming community which it served. It was a five-month term, with two and one-half months in the summer and two and one-half months in the winter between planting and harvesting. The building, which was destroyed by fire in 1914 and never replaced, was erected by the people in the community and the name derived from the Lunsford family of the Miles Lunsford clan. Among the early families were the Abe Lunsfords, John Lunsfords, and Bed Lunsfords.

K. K. Houston taught at the school in 1910 when the school was nicknamed "Seed Tick Chapel." There were about 40 students at this time. Other early teachers were Bob Long, Arthur Spencer, Will Raney, and Hurst Jennings.

The first school at Bath Springs was constructed during the 1860s, a log structure located just across from the present Dr. B. M. Brooks home. In 1913 the building was torn down and a yellow pine school building erected about 50 feet from the present Bath Springs Baptist Church. It was used as a school-church combination until 1929 when Three Way School was built. George Brooks was one of the early teachers.

Rocky Springs School was built on land owned by Green Miller. Located three and one-half miles north of Jeanette, the first building was a one-room boxed building. This building was torn down and a new building erected in 1929. Faye Jordan Dailey taught the first two years of the new school. Other teachers who taught were Dora McMurry, Beulah Anderson, Maude Morgan, Hurst Jennings, Marlin Dodd, Lerah Jordan Rains, Joe Quinn, Barbara Bowman, Camilla Odle, Olis Quinn, George Mays, Sam B. Baker, Lounell Rainey, Ola Smith, Ireland Oxford, Ottis Dodd, Edward Hearington, and Mary Inman. With consolidation of county schools, this school closed its doors, and Mr. and Mrs. Edwin Gibson bought the building and remodeled it for their home.

In Decaturville about 1909, a school building was erected on the Perryville-Decaturville Road. It was destroyed by the only tornado ever to hit Decaturville to date and was replaced by a brick structure in 1911. In 1928, an annex was added and was connected by a walkway. One building was used for a grammar school and the other for a high school. Later, during WPA days, a gymnasium was also constructed near the school with WPA labor.

The first school in Parsons was a one-room, 40 x 60 feet, frame building, located at the corner of Tennessee Avenue and Fifth Street, at the present site of the G. L. Colwick home. The building, constructed by Ollie and Ike Buckner, had a petition dividing the beginners and older students. A stage graced the west end of the building where school plays were presented.

One of the schools of higher learning in Decatur County was the Parsons University. The red brick structure, located on West Third Street, behind the present Parsons Elementary School, was

Parsons University in 1908.

built in 1908 by private stock holders for $5000. Shares were sold for $1 each and ran from $25 to $100. They were not redeemable. Civic-minded citizens of Parsons helped solicit funds to build the university which replaced the first school in Parsons. Included in the new school building were two large rooms, a music room and downstairs office, with the auditorium and stage and two dressing rooms upstairs.

Teachers were paid according to the number of students that attended since it was a subscription school where each pupil paid tuition. The higher grade students paid $2.50 a month, while lower grade students had to pay $1.50 tuition each month. Jim Wheat was one of the teachers, and subjects taught under his tutoring were equivalent to first-year college. The school became an official high school, supported by state and county funds in 1915.

In 1923 the inadequacy of the small building for a high school became apparent, and the mayor and board of aldermen began action which would more than double the facilities to accomodate the growing need. With a $15,000 bond issue, the extension was built onto the back of the former building. Included was an auditorium with a stage and comfortable opera chairs. A gymnasium was added in 1930. This building, which began as Parsons University and which became Parsons High School, served the town until 1948 when a new high school was constructed at 303 Hill Street.

By 1929 almost every community in Decatur County had a school. There were 53 one-teacher schools, four two-teacher schools, and four three-teacher or more schools. Only two of these, one at Parsons and one at Decaturville, were high schools. Even as late as 1945, there were still 41 schools in the county, most of them still one-teacher operations.

However, between 1945 and 1950 a process of consolidation began. There were several causes. Many families moved to cities for better paying jobs. More prosperous families sent their children to town schools where better educational advantages were available. The subsequent drop in already small enrollments in the rural schools forced many of them to close since they could not meet state attendance requirements. The final death blow to the small schools came with the beginning of school bus service. Most parents living in the rural areas wanted their children to attend grammar school in town schools, and school buses made that possible.

The consolidation process continued until in 1975 there were only five schools in Decatur County: Parsons Junior High, Parsons Elementary, Riverside Consolidated High School, Decaturville Elementary, and Scotts Hill. However, only a small number of students at Scotts Hill are Decatur Countians since the county line runs through the middle of the school and both Henderson and Decatur Countians enroll there. The former high school in Parsons, built in 1948, is presently serving as Parsons Junior High School. In 1956 Parsons Elementary School was built on the campus of the former Parsons University. The Decaturville Elementary School was erected in 1957.

A most controversial action was the merging of Decaturville High School and Parsons High School into Riverside Consolidated High School. Plans were formulated as early as 1963 for consolidation when the school board voted favorably for the project. When it was put to a vote by the citizens of the county, consolidation won by 18 votes.

The new school was built halfway between the two towns on what was once known as the "Turn Pike." Constructed by H. D. Pevahouse Construction Company at a cost of $536,000, it covers 77,000 square feet. The building has nine classrooms and 20 teaching stations. The rooms are equipped for television sets and other modern teaching aids.

Physical conditions and educational climate have improved considerably in Decatur County from the days of the one-room, one-teacher schools. The county has always made the most of its educational opportunities. It was the first county in the region to become a part of the Kentucky Dam Library Region. This was in October of 1942 and was sponsored by TVA. Roy N. McPeake was named the first chairman of the seven member library board for Decatur, and he has served as board chairman since that date. Branch book stations were set up at various locations to furnish reading material to Decatur Countians.

The county library was first located in the office of the superintendent of education in the courthouse. Around 1955, the library was moved from the courthouse to a building on the south side of the square. Later it was moved back to the courthouse. The library now occupies an air-conditioned room on the first floor of the courthouse. Marie Smith was appointed as first librarian. After she resigned, Grace Vise was appointed and served until her retirement in November of 1976. Mrs. E. H. Wylie was appointed to succeed Mrs. Vise and began serving as librarian on December 1, 1976.

Through all the years of change in education in Decatur County, including the upheaval of integration in the 1950s which was achieved without violence or interruption of normal school service, the one constant fact has been dedicated teachers and concerned community leaders who have faced the problems and have sought the right direction. The following lists, by no means complete, name those involved.

Early Teachers

Among the early teachers of the county were Elias Blount, familiarly known as Governor Blount, Elisa Deaton, George W. Beard, Green B. Rushing, W. M. Dalton, B. H. Southerland, John Tinker, Milt Houston, Hyder Smith, Nattie Fisher, John Tucker, J. C. Duck, B. A. Tucker, Mrs. George Bell, and John McIllwain.

Decatur County Superintendents

Among those who have served as school superintendent were the following: B. A. Tucker, 1891-1893; W. H. McMillan, 1893-1897; B. A. Tucker, 1889-1901; H. W. Long, 1901-1903; Jake Miller, 1903-1907; Jim Wheat, 1907-1909; George L. Wortham, Sr., 1911-1915; Perry Murphy, 1915-1916; George L. Wortham, Sr., 1916-1922; Ray Holley, 1922-1925; J. K. Vise, 1925-1931; R. L. Haney, 1931-1935; K. K. Houston, 1935-1939; W. C. White, 1941; C. A. Palmer, 1941-1945; Jack Stevens, 1945-1948; Guy Kennedy, 1948-1960; Edward Hearington, 1960-1968; Henry Evans, 1968-1969. Evans died while in office, and he was succeeded by his wife, Iris A. Evans, who served from 1969 until 1970, when Billy Stevens was elected. He served from 1970 until 1976. Wayne Stanfill was elected in 1976. His term expires in 1980.

Natural Wonders

The extensive limestone deposits in Decatur County have not only added to the industrial material, they have provided the natural wonder of caves. Through ages of water erosion, the limestone has dissolved leaving cavernous fissures inside the earth. Today these caves still excite the imagination and offer adventure to the brave explorer.

One such cave is known as Baugus Cave and is located on Highway 69 six miles north of Parsons. The cave is topped with layer after layer of limestone rock formation and has a wide opening at the mouth. There is a walkable ceiling, but after passing three rooms, it becomes necessary to crawl. Water drips into the cave at various points. There are six rooms reaching a quarter of a mile in distance.

Baugus Cave became highly publicized in 1928 when two men from Waverly, Tennessee, attempted to explore the cave. One of them, while crawling in the rooms, got hung in a crevice. Excitement went on a rampage. An S.O.S. reached the town of Parsons late in the afternoon, and a large crowd gathered at the mouth of the cave. Volunteers worked until midnight before rescuing the victim, safe and sound, except from shock.

Another cave in the county was first known as the Elzar Burton Cave; however, it is now known as Featherfoot Cave. Located north of the Alvin C. York Bridge near Perryville, it was named for Sam Burton's grandfather who came to this country from Virginia in 1825. Burton returned to Virginia and moved to what was then called Perry County, on the west side of the Tennessee River. He bought 5000 acres of land which extended to the river.

This cave has had many names. Elzar Burton sold it to a Mr. Anders, and the name was changed to Anders Cave. In 1885 Anders sold it to Captain Alley, and he named it Alley's Cave. Before Alley died, Sam Burton purchased it in 1926.

A few people have inhabited the cave. Two men, a Mr. Thomas from Bridgeport, Alabama, lived there for 18 months, and later Bill Ripley and his wife and children, lived there for two

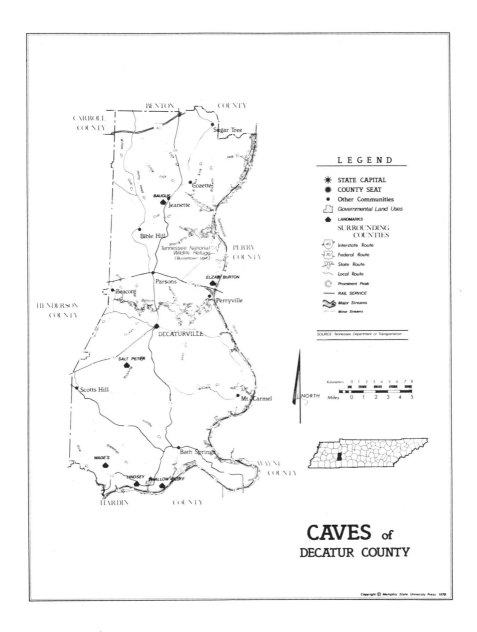

LEGEND

✳ STATE CAPITAL
◉ COUNTY SEAT
● Other Communities
Governmental Land Uses
♦ LANDMARKS
SURROUNDING COUNTIES
40 Interstate Route
70 Federal Route
State Route
Local Route
Prominent Peak
RAIL SERVICE
Major Streams
Minor Streams

SOURCE Tennessee Department of Transportation

Kilometers 0 1 2 3 4 5 6 7 8
Miles 0 1 2 3 4 5

NORTH

CAVES of
DECATUR COUNTY

years. He was nicknamed "Featherfoot," the source of the present day name of the cave.

Despite the fact that only two families have lived in the cave, many who came down the river stayed there overnight. Some were fugitives and others unknown. The cave was also used by deserters as a hideout during the Civil War. It can be reached only by water amid the rock wall of the Tennessee River.

Featherfoot Cave has one big room 20 by 25 feet. Other rooms have narrow openings, and one must crawl to get through. There are deep crevices with streams running through them to the old Sam Burton place. In the back of the cave one can hear traffic on the highway.

The Lindsey Cave is located 15 miles south of Decaturville near Cedar Bluff. It received its name from Lindsey Yarbro who discovered about 85 years ago a newborn baby that had died in the cave. The rock entrance, a very low opening, leads to several rooms. One large, wide room has a big hole of water in it.

Another cave is Wade's Cave, located on the James Earl Wade farm 13 miles southwest of Decaturville on Stewman Creek. This cave is about 80 feet long and has several rooms.

A cave at Swallow Bluff, known as the Swallow Bluff Cave, is located about 14 miles south of Decaturville on the Tennessee River. It has one large room which extends about 800 yards. About halfway through this cave is a hill that has been named "Tator Hill" because the rock formations on it look like small potatoes. One has to cross over Tator Hill to go all the way through the cave. One other cave in the county is Salt Peter Cave, about a half mile long, located four miles southwest of Decaturville.

Architectural Landmarks

The early architecture for houses in the county was the basic pioneer one-room log cabin. Sometimes a second room was added with an open hallway, or "dogtrot," separating the two.

Two-story houses also were built, the upstairs usually being one big room for sleeping. Chimneys, often built at both ends of the house, were used for heating and cooking. Open porches, both front and back, afforded shade and the opportunity to catch cooling breezes.

One of the earliest structures still standing in the county is the "Old Shannon Place" in Bath Springs. Bob Shannon came to West Tennessee from North Carolina and crossed the Tennessee River at what was then known as Carrolville and entered land here in the untamed country. Indians were living in the territory at the time. Local conjecture dates the construction of the house around 1795.

The house, built of yellow poplar logs and chinked with mud, had two limestone chimneys. There were two large front rooms downstairs and a dogtrot that led to the dining room and kitchen out back, and one large room upstairs. Wooden shutters served as windows.

An amusing incident concerning the place is reported to have happened during the Civil War. Union soldiers, camping near the Shannon house at Tanyard hollow, looted the Shannon house of its silver, cooking utensils, meat, and lard, and carried it to their camp. A friend of the family by the name of Mrs. Murphy pretended to be a Yankee woman and persuaded the men to give her the silver and utensils since she was needy. She returned them to the Shannon family.

The home remained in the Shannon family until 1901, the last one to live there being John Shannon, the grandfather of Jess Robert Lancaster who lives at 111 East Ninth Street in Parsons. Lancaster's mother, Flora Shannon, was married at the Shannon home in 1900 to Edd Lancaster.

John Shannon sold the old homeplace to Samp Russ in 1901. Russ rented the place out. Those living there through the years have been Will Davidson, Bud Stafford, Henry Yarbro, and R. C. McCutchen. Alton Mays purchased the Shannon place about 1913 and remodeled it. It is now weatherboarded and has been in the Mays family since that date.

The Red House, an early stage coach stop, is another pioneer building of historical importance. Located 15 miles south of Decaturville just off Highway 69 near Bath Springs, the house was built in 1805 of yellow poplar, hand-hewn logs with chimneys of limestone, one of which is intact. The two-story structure has one big room, hallway, kitchen, dining room, and back porch on the ell with smoke house adjoining. Upstairs has one big room with homemade beds nailed to the wall.

It received the name "Red House" because it was painted red. One of the first families to live there was the Sparks, who presumedly built the house. The land has been in the Martin family for about 85 years. It is presently owned by L. D. Martin and R. M. Martin.

The Red House Cemetery, only a short distance from the house, was first called Akin Cemetery. Here slaves are buried as well as many persons from pioneer days. The cemetery is still being used. An early grave is Samuel Sparks, born 1755, died 1811. The Hancock pioneer family are also buried here.

The antebellum "Townsend House" is a picturesque colonial structure perched on a hill overlooking a crest of fertile farm land and green pastures. It is located about one mile east of Parsons on the old Perryville road. Formerly a two-story log house, chinked with mud, it was built during the 1830s by Ural Rushing. The house has belonged to many persons, including Rennie Rains, Leslie R. Rains, B. H. Maxwell, Joe Jordan, E. M. Townsend, and Wilburn Townsend. It is presently owned by Mr. and Mrs. David Yarbro.

Another landmark is the former home of Mr. and Mrs. J. T. Smith, located ten miles east of Decaturville near Brownsport Furnace. The stately two-story colonial structure is perched high on a hill overlooking the Tennessee River. Constructed in 1897, the house has ten rooms, two halls, four porches, and five fireplaces.

Lumber for the construction was shipped by boat on the Tennessee River, and only the best grade lumber was used. It was a true showplace in its day. The verandas had banisters of intricate design which were easily visible on the white weatherboard house. The house's water supply came from two cisterns, one at the edge of the front porch and the other at the back porch edge. Water was caught from the roof of the house in the V-trough of the big cistern.

In 1915 it became the home of Mr. and Mrs. Coy E. White. Of their eight children, four were born there: Kate, George William, Josephine Herndon, and Martha Ann Pettigrew. Presently the once stately mansion stands alone, weatherbeaten, unoccupied, and falling down. It is owned by George William White.

The Dr. B. M. Brooks home, located in the heart of Bath Springs, was built when Dr. Brooks moved from Turnbow Creek in 1900 and began his practice in Bath Springs. Located 300 yards due west of Hancock's famous summer resort, the structure has seven rooms and two halls. There are two porches, one on the front and one on the back. It was the first two-story house to be built in the Bath Springs Community.

This landmark has been in the original family since its construction. Dr. and Mrs. Brooks were the parents of three sons: Martin, Walter Kendrick, and Erskine, who died as a youth. There were also three daughters: Blanche Turner, Flavius Alexander, and Mae Horner. Presently it is occupied by Blanche Turner and Martin Brooks.

One of the original landmarks in Decatur County, located in Parsons, is the Colwick Building, last occupied by Glennie Colwick. It was built by John P. Rains, father of Stella Jennings. The two-story brick building housed a hotel and general mercantile store in the early days. One side was used for dry goods and the other for groceries. The rear of the store and upstairs was used for a hotel. Constructed of brick made at a brick kiln on the ground, it was completed in 1898. It was a nightly attraction for persons to drop by and watch the process of brick making at the kiln. When the building was completed, a big ball was held.

The Colwicks operated the hotel until 1934. Among the other operators were Ethel Duck and Reba Duck. At one time Sid Bawcum operated a grocery store in one side of the building.

When Rains moved to Memphis in 1919, he sold the building and business to J. T. Colwick. Later it was sold to W. D. Colwick. After the death of W. D. Colwick in 1938 his son, Glennie, operated the business until his death in 1973. After the death of Glennie Colwick, the building was sold to Farmers Bank which still owns it. Vernon R. Hill & Son Tile Company is presently located in the landmark.

The white weatherboard home of the late George Washington Baugus was considered a mansion at the turn of the century in Decatur County. Located on an 800-acre farm near Jeanette, the two-story, twelve-room structure could be seen for miles around. The home had a Corinthian portico, mahogany double front door, and 12 carved rock mantels.

It was in 1890 that the house was constructed for the Baugus family by Ike and Ollie Buckner with lumber from the 500 acre tract of timber on the land. George Washington Baugus and wife, Emily Lucendy Grey Baugus, moved there with their family when the house was completed. The once spacious mansion deteriorated quickly when the family left. It was rented for a while but stood unoccupied prior to its destruction by fire in 1964.

Newspapers

The first newspaper published in the county was the *Decatur County Beacon.* It was edited by Dan Barry, and the first copy came out on September 10, 1881. Unfortunately, Barry died in November of 1881.

On the 14th day of April, 1881, Charlie, Frank, and W. V. Barry arrived in Decaturville. It was here that W. V. Barry launched his newspaper career. He ran the *Decatur County Beacon* without any help except that of Reverend Tom P. Ramsey, pastor of the Southern Methodist Church. Reverend Ramsey was a boyhood friend of W. V. Barry's father, Dr. Dan Barry. He manipulated the hand rollers to distribute the ink on the forms while the editor pulled the lever of the Washington hand press.

The newspaper was published weekly at a cost of only one dollar a year. In the issue dated July 12, 1883, the editor printed the following special offer:

> 'To Getters Up of Clubs' We will send the *Beacon* free for six months to anyone who will send us three names in the county accompanied by $3 in cash. To anyone sending five names, accompanied by $5 in cash, we will give a free year's subscription and to anyone who brings us 50 names with $50 we will give $5 in cash.

In 1892 Henry Barry joined his uncle in the newspaper field in Decaturville. The name of the paper was changed to the *Decatur County Herald,* and the newspaper remained in the Barry family for 61 years. The last publishers of the Barry clan were Iris King of Decaturville and her husband, Lonnie King. They published the newspaper until 1961, when it was sold to Bill Craddock and Jarvis Williams of Savannah. Later, the *Decatur County Herald* was purchased by the Parsons Printing Corporation, and today the *Decatur County Herald* and the *Parsons News Leader* form one county newspaper.

The second county newspaper was known as the *Parsons Pioneer,* published by G. S. (Sterling) Barry and D. D. Deason. The newspaper continued to operate peacefully until August 18, 1893, when the editors dissolved partnership. Here is an account of the transaction:

> On Monday morning last the *Pioneer* taken its departure for Greenfield, Tenn. in the hands of G. W. Walters where he expects to run a newspaper. We were sorry to see it leave for it was a newsy little sheet and highly respected by its readers. We are not willing to do without a paper, it would seem like a member of the family had forever left us, so we are going to supply its place with *The Messenger.*

In 1900 the little newspaper changed its name once again from the *Parsons Messenger* to the *Parsons Journal.*

From 1901 until 1905 Parsons had two newspapers, *The Tennessee River Wave,* which was published only a short time by a Mr. Petus, and the *Parsons Journal.* The *Parsons Journal* changed hands several times, before finally ceasing publication.

Parsons was without a paper in 1925 when J. C. Partin started what is now known as the *Parsons News Leader.* He bought the equipment from Barry, which had been used in printing the *Parsons Journal.* Later Partin's son, Jim, took over the paper and ran it until 1952 when Edwin Townsend purchased it and continued publication with Max Townsend as editor. In 1963 it became the Parsons Printing Corporation, owned and operated by Mr. and Mrs. Max Townsend.

Citizens of Decaturville were without a newspaper until 1965 when Everett Baker of Adamsville began the *Decatur County News-Graphic.* Bill Akers later became publisher and then sold the paper to George M. Hamilton at Selmer, who continued the publication under the name of the *Decatur County Independent.* Bill Crossnoe served as editor in 1967. He was succeeded by Lerah Washam, who served as editor until the paper was discontinued in September, 1967. Today Decatur County has one newspaper, *Parsons News Leader* and *Decatur County Herald* combination.

Medical Services

There were 16 doctors listed in the 1850 census of Decatur County. Other early doctors established practices in the county. John Parsons, located in Parsons, served as treasurer of the Board of Health of Decatur County in the 1870s. Troy W. Jones was a practitioner at Decaturville. A native of Henderson County, he began the study of medicine under the preceptorship of Dr. G. H. Derryberry, and afterwards under Dr. Tryar.

J. N. Houston, son of John L. and Jane Graham Houston, was born in Decatur County, January 22, 1837. He was educated in the college at Decaturville and attended lectures in Nashville in 1856-1857. In the summer of 1857 he began the practice of medicine in Perry County at Brown's Mills. About five months later, he returned to Decatur County.

At the outbreak of the Civil War he enlisted with the 52nd Tennessee Regiment of the Confederate army under the command of Colonel B. J. Lee and served as assistant surgeon of the regiment at the battle of Shiloh. After 12 months service, he returned to his home county of Decatur.

William G. Rains was born October 26, 1837. He began his study of medicine under Dr. J. H. Hill and Dr. J. H. Leonard of Decaturville and completed his course at the Nashville University in 1867. Practicing medicine first at Sulphur Springs, he moved to Decaturville in 1868. From Decaturville, he moved to Parsons where he served until his death.

George Brasher served as sheriff of Decatur County for two terms prior to becoming a doctor. He graduated from the University of Tennessee in 1909 and spent nearly 10 years in the Tennessee River hill country in the north end of Decatur County and the south end of Benton, covering the rugged territory on horseback or by buggy.

Robert Wylie was born in Decatur County, September 21, 1877, son of Mr. and Mrs. John Wylie. He received his education in the county, later graduating from the University of Tennessee in 1906. He practiced at Scotts Hill until 1958. He gave invaluable service to a wide rural area and was honored on his 50th medical anniversary with a "Dr. Wylie Day." His son, Paul Wylie, also became a doctor and practiced in Jackson, Tennessee, until his retirement.

David E. Hill, born near Bible Hill in 1852, received his training at Vanderbilt University. He rode horseback to visit his patients, with medicine in saddle bags. His price for delivering a baby was from $5 to $7.50 according to the financial condition of the family. Ordinary visits were $1; however, if he passed another doctor's home en route, the price jumped to $2. He practiced medicine in Decatur County for almost a half-century until his death in 1918.

Other early doctors include William B. Keeton at Decaturville; John T. Keeton at Vise Town, later moving to Saltillo and on to Clifton; James A. Allen at Turnbow Creek until 1893 when he moved to Trenton, Tennessee; B. M. Brooks at Bath Springs until his death in 1929; and Gabe Lancaster at Dunbar.

Among the doctors who settled at Sugar Tree were J. E. Martin, Jimmy Batten, J. E. Ingram, James D. Bradley, Byrd Barnett, and John Flatte. R. Y. Fisher practiced medicine in Decaturville, as did J. G. McMillan, Tab Rogers, Hurbert Conger, and Pete Conger.

Among those who were listed in the 70th session of the Tennessee State Medical Association in 1903 were W. G. Rains, who was president of Decatur County Medical Association; Ed Bostic, Parsons; R. Y. Fisher and J. G. McMillan, Decaturville; R. M. Brown, Bible Hill; L. C. Gates, Vise Town; E. G. Howell, Swallow Bluff; and J. W. Montgomery, Thurman. James Logan McMillan, son of Dr. J. G. McMillan, began his practice in Decaturville shortly after his father's retirement and continued until his death in 1937. Twentieth century physicians in Decatur County include J. E. Ingram, L. E. Luna, John N. McAnerny, Edward Cutshaw, Max Ray Wyatt, Jasper Bray, C. H. Chafee, Alonzo Dickson, A. G. Hufstedler, and Pete Conger.

Paul Ford Teague came to Decatur County in 1962 and started a clinic. Assisting him in the clinic was Joe Wilhite. Robert Fisher joined Dr. Teague in 1964. After Paul Ford Teague began practice in Parsons, plans were formulated to construct the first hospital in the county. The plans became a reality when Decatur County General Hospital was dedicated in December of 1963, and the first patient, Toka Phillips, was admitted on December 8, 1963. The 22-bed hospital was financed by the taxpayers of Decatur County without any federal aid and is owned and operated by the county.

Members serving on the hospital board were Joe Gregory, Sr., chairman, H. L. Townsend, Sr., secretary and treasurer, Fred Alexander, vice-chairman, and Kenneth Graves, Bob White, Delmar Ballinger, and George W. White. After Paul Ford Teague resigned from the hospital staff and moved to Memphis in 1969, Charles Alderson of Memphis joined the staff in 1970. George Shannon and Jimmy Meeks joined the staff in 1974. On April 3, 1967, Decatur County Court voted to issue bonds to finance a 14-bed additional space to the hospital. When the new $124,000 addition was completed, it doubled the size of the hospital and increased the patient capacity to 37.

Wars

Decatur County was divided concerning the Civil War. There were 310 votes cast for separation and 550 votes against separation. There was no such thing as neutral ground, and few able-bodied men escaped the army.

The first troops raised for the Confederate service were the company of Captain Isham G. Hearn. This company became the 27th Tennessee C.S.A. It was called the Decatur County Tigers, and the regiment was organized at Trenton in 1861 by the election of C. H. Williams, colonel, B. H. Brown, lieutenant colonel, and Samuel Love, major. Hearn's death occurred at Shiloh, April 6, 1862.

Jonathan Luton raised the second company in the county which was as a part of the 31st C. S. A. (West Tennessee) Regiment. The officers of the regiment were Colonel A. H. Bradford, Lieutenant Colonel C. M. Cason, and Major John Smith. Four companies were raised for the 52nd Tennessee Regiment C. S. A. by N. A. Wesson, W. R. Akin, J. H. Thomas, and John McMillan. Commissioned officers of the last company were J. L. Tuck, P. R. Brasher, S. L. McClure, John Esle, and J. C. Rundle.

Decatur County furnished two companies for the Federal army. The first raised was by Captain Elisha Roberts in October of 1862. Roberts, William Chandler, and William C. Webb were captains of this company. They formed the Sixth Union Regiment Tennessee Cavalry.

The second Union regiment was the Tennessee Mounted Infantry raised by Andrew Roberts. The nucleus of this regiment was Company A, which was mustered into service October 1, 1863. By February 1, 1864, the regiment numbered seven companies. The operations of this cavalry regiment were mainly in doing fort duty, scouting the country in picking up stragglers, and preventing recruiting for the Confederacy.

Being isolated from the great lines of travel, except for the Tennessee River, Decatur County was comparatively free from the march of the armies. However, a skirmish did occur on Nebo Hill near Red House, an old stage coach stop. It is reported that a stray shot hit a man who was working in a field nearby. He was carried to the Red House. His blood stained the wall of the living room and stairway and remained there until 1915 when it was painted over. It has been considered a haunted house, and those living there earlier reported that they could hear horses being ungeared in the yard and the gears thrown in the hall and voices outside.

During the conflict, General Forrest used the landing at Perryville as a crossing for his army. After the gunboat battle at Johnsonville, part of the army ferried to the east side of the river. General Forrest also came through Perryville on his way to Jackson. His men followed the old Sardis Road, cutting their trail wide enough for the horses and wagons to travel.

An interesting story of a soldier who fought on both sides is that of John M. Countess. He enlisted in the 16th Tennessee Confederate Army under the command of John Savage. He fought in the battles of Huttonville and the Chute Mountains, Virginia. He later enlisted in the Fifth Tennessee Cavalry of the Union Army.

Another Decatur Countian who fought for both the Union and the Confederacy was H. M. Jordan. He enlisted in the Confederate army under the command of Colonel B. J. Lee and took part in the battle of Shiloh. After one year of faithful service, he returned home where he remained for about six months and then enlisted in the Federal service and was attached to the 2nd Tennessee Regiment under the command of Colonel Murphy.

Although not divisive nor as devastating as the effects of the Civil War, World War I and World War II once again brought suffering and hardship into the lives of Decatur Countians. The departure of fathers and sons created painful upheavals in family life. Shortages of such items as grain, sugar, and fuel forced sacrifices on the homefront. The ultimate sacrifice, however, was made by those who were killed on the battlefields.

A marker is placed on the lawn of the Decatur County Courthouse in Decaturville with the names of World War I veterans on one side and the names of World War II veterans on the other side who died for their country. Listed at the top of the marker are these words: "Dedicated to the everlasting memory of those in Decatur County who gave their lives in the service of their country." Killed in the Korean conflict were James F. Hamm and Frank P. Jennings. Again war touched the lives of Decatur Countians when American involvement in Vietnam began to escalate in the 1960s. Men who participated in this war were:

Jerry Adisson
Freddie Jean Bartholomew
Henry Bawcum
Jack Bawcum
Robert Bawcum
Vernon L. Benthal
Gene W. Bledsoe
Denver H. Bowman
Randall J. Cagle
Wayne Cagle
John H. Campbell
Harvey Cotham
Richard Cotham
Lester R. Davis
Robert Dickson
Fredie A. Fisher
Roy Gibbons, Jr.
J. W. Perry
Clifford Henry Pettit, Jr.

Johnnie Gibson
Mac Arthur Gibson
Michael Griggs
Joe Griggs
David Inman
Tony P. Johnson
Jimmy Jones
Eugene King
Jerry W. Lee
Billy Lomax
Jimmy H. Long
Colin K. Mathis
Edward Milton Mathis
Garney Mathis
Jerry Lynn Miller
Logan Patterson
James Robert Perkins
William Taylor
Jerry Paul Teague

Eli Michael Pettit
Lewis C. Pratt
James R. Raney
Jerry Wayne Rosson
Donald A. Ruiz
Eugene R. Scott
William H. Simpson
W. C. Sims
Bunes Smith
Don R. Smith
William Clyde Smith
Bob Stivers
Guy Lynn Stokes

Steven W. Tolley
Bryan Gene Townsend
Buddy Tuten
Roger D. Tuten
Vernon Veazey
Jodie Warren
Harold Dean Weatherford
Clyde Wisham
Royal Wood
Garry S. Yarbro
Mike Yarbro
Tony O. Yates
Boyd Lee Young

Monument of those who gave their lives for their country in World War I and World War II, on the lawn of Decaturville Courthouse, placed there by the American Legion and the V.F.W.

Tennessee State Guard

The Tennessee State Guard was created by Chapter 15, Public Act of the State of Tennessee, 1941, for the purpose of replacing the national guard, which was being mobilized in World War II. The Fourth Provisional Company was organized in Decatur County on April 28, 1942, and reached full strength and was duly commissioned as an active company on November 16, 1942. The first officers of the company were G. Tillman Stewart as captain; Arthur F. Tolley as first lieutenant; Audrey Plautt Maxwell, Ernest Sylvester Yates, and Walter Eugene McPeak as second lieutenants; Leonard O. Townsend as top sergeant; Harold White as supply sergeant; and Hobart L. Townsend as company clerk.

There were 120 in the company at the beginning, composed of men ages 16 to 60 throughout Decatur County. According to an annual federal inspection report of the company on April 18, 1946, 60 of the original men in the company had gone into the armed forces of World War II. A total of 42 men remained in the company on April 18, 1946.

When World War II ended, the Tennessee State Guard was ordered demobilized. The complete dissolution of the Fourth Provisional Company of Parsons was effective April 15, 1947, at which time Captain Hobart L. Townsend was promoted to Major by Governor Jim Nance McCord. In the 1950s, Decatur County again provided soldiers, this time for the "police action" in Korea.

Towns

Decaturville, County Seat

The county seat, located in the south central portion of Decatur County, was deeded to Samuel McLead, Samuel Brasher, Balsam Jones, and David B. Funderburk on May 7, 1847. Twenty-five acres were purchased from John McMillan, and ten acres were purchased from Burrell Rushing.

Lots were sold just after the town plot was laid out. Purchasers were Pettigrew and Coats, John Garrett, L. C. Friendly, Daniel McLead, P. H. Fisher, E. E. Tate, Lawson Kelley, E. E. Jones, John McMillan, W. H. Bennett, J. W. Delaney, G. N. Gains, and H. C. Frayers.

The first court met in Decaturville in 1848 in a cabin on the west side of the square. This was used only a short time until the erection of a two-story frame courthouse, which burned July 3, 1869, with all the records except those in the register's office and the clerk and master's office. It was claimed that the fire was the work of an arsonist for the purpose of destroying the records.

On July 12, 1869, a committee composed of J. W. Mayo, W. C. Frayer, and D. M. Scott was appointed to submit plans and specifications for a new courthouse. The committee went to work at once, and the contract was let in October for a two-story brick structure at a cost of $9,000. The first floor contained offices for the county officials, and the second floor was designed for court proceedings.

Once again Decatur County courthouse was destroyed by fire in 1927. Again it was thought by the general public to be the work of an arsonist for the same purpose of destroying the records. All records were destroyed with the exception of the ones in the county court clerk's, register's, and clerk and master's offices. After this fire, county offices were moved to the Eli Vise store, a two-story building located on the southeast corner of court square, which was destroyed by fire in 1968, and court was held in the Decaturville School building.

A crash building program went into effect to build a new courthouse and in less than 12 months, a fireproof, brick and concrete structure was completed. On the building committee were J. A. Chalk, chairman, V. A. Lancaster, R. E. Spence, W. S. Dennison, and J. W. Blount who served as secretary and treasurer. Elston Tate was architect and contractor, and Fount Tate served as foreman. The courthouse underwent a face-lifting in 1975 when Hardin Smith was elected to serve as county judge. A complete renovation with additional offices created from space unused in the basement offered not only an eye-catching effect but much needed space. The cost amounted to $200,000 which included painting many of the rooms.

After the division of Perry County, the new county of Decatur was allowed to use the jail and court square in Perryville for public purposes until a new site could be selected and a new building erected. However, it was not long before a jail was built in Decaturville. Located one block east of the court square, it was constructed of logs and bricks and served the county until 1885, when it was destroyed by fire.

A replica of the old jail was constructed. A committee in 1868 reported this jail badly in need of repair, but no definite action was taken until 1883 when J. W. Wiley, J. C. Hardin, and W. B. Fisher were appointed to supervise the erection of a new jail. Their report was filed April 7, 1884, and a new jail was ordered. According to records, the new jail was described thus, "The cells are of the most improved pattern and are deemed entirely safe." The whole cost amounted to around $9,000 and included an attached sheriff's residence.

When this jail gave way and the steel work rusted, it was replaced by a new one-story concrete block structure in 1961. The bonds were sold under the administration of Judge James Long, who died before the building was erected, and his wife, Judge Juanita Long, completed the transaction. A $60,000 bond issue was floated with $19,000 earmarked for the Decatur County Nursing Home, $11,000 for the sheriff's house, and $30,000 for the jail.

The first post office to serve this area was the Beech River Post Office established March 1, 1847. Serving as first postmaster was Amos M. Yarbro. On September 20, 1847, David McLead was appointed to serve as postmaster, and the name of the post office was changed to Decaturville.

Besides being the headquarters of county government, Decaturville also became an early business center. Gilbert McMillan, listed as the first settler in Decaturville, had a business dating back to 1836 which was known as McMillan's Shop. Another early settler was Daniel McLead, who built a log cabin

Duncan Mercantile, 1945. Early business place in Decaturville.

on the northeast corner of court square where Decatur County Bank is now located. He carried a line of general merchandise. Staples included barrels of flour, sugar, unground coffee, New Orleans sorghum, and whiskey. When the Smith Hotel, which was built around the log cabin, was torn away for the new bank building in 1966, the cabin was discovered intact, and the logs have been preserved.

Samuel Yarbro and Jonathan Luton were the first dry goods merchants. Later, Young and Johnson opened a business on the southeast corner of the square. Others locating in the county seat town were J. J. Sharp Company; Young, Stern and Smith; J. M. Fryar; Kendrick and Roberts; and, Blythe and Beuodrant.

The Chrisenberry Hotel, located one block north of the court square, at the present location of Edgar Hobbs residence, was one of the first of its kind in Decaturville. It was a story and a half frame structure and catered mostly to boarders, which included students who attended school at Decaturville Academy. It was operated by Gooch Chrisenberry's father.

About five years later, John Bray built a hotel, located on the northeast corner of court square, where Decatur County Bank is now located, and operated it until 1880. It was first known as "The Bray House." In 1880, Mr. and Mrs. Curry P. Dennison took over the hotel, and it became known as "The Dennison House." Mr. and Mrs. Joseph Smith became operators of the Dennison House about 1900, and the name was changed to the "Smith Hotel." The two-story frame, verandaed building was torn down in 1966 to make room for a new Decatur County Bank building.

The Decatur County Bank, chartered in 1899 and capitalized at $5000, was the first bank in Decaturville. The original incorporators were Rube Smith, who served as the first cashier, Judge James A. England, who later served as president, and Judge John E. McCall, Jr., E. J. Timberlake and H. E. Graper, all of Lexington. Judge McCall, who was a circuit judge at the time, was later named a federal judge. Timberlake was a prominent landowner of Henderson County, and Graper was cashier of the Citizens Bank of Lexington.

The first president was P. W. Miller, who served as clerk and master of Decatur County for many years. J. F. Dees served as president of the bank from 1929 until 1972. He was succeeded by Paul Simmons, who served until his death in 1973, and in turn was succeeded by Grady Dixon.

The Decaturville and Scotts Hill Funeral Homes had their origin in the Peoples Burial Association, organized in Decaturville in 1921 by W. T. Hopper, who rode horseback throughout Decatur and surrounding counties soliciting members for J. T. Smith and Company who operated the funeral homes. Not only is the Peoples Burial Association the oldest burial association in the state, but it was the first association of its kind east of the Mississippi River.

Business places listed in Decaturville in 1976 were Central Service Station, Decaturville Truck and Trailer, Decatur Tractor & Implement Co., Mid-Way Truck Stop, Decaturville Feed Mill, Decaturville Lumber Co., 83 Service Station, Times Theatre, U. S. S. Agriculture Chemical Co., Decaturville Foodland, Larry's Exxon Station, Decatur Farmers Co-op, Decatur County Machinery Co., Smith's Grocery, F & P Food Market, White and Smith, Style Shoppe, Mid-Way Cafe, Down Town Bar and Grill, B & K Dry Goods Co., Vise Garage, Dorothy's Shoppe, Crawley's Auto Parts, Vic's Dollar Store, Variety Shoppe, Thrift Shop, Jack's Factory Outlet, King's Furniture, Lunsford Pharmacy, Peggy's Dress Shop, Times Cafe, Crawley's Furniture Co., White's Cafe, Decaturville Funeral Home, The Harmony House, Betty's Beauty Shop, Patty's Beauty Shop, Nellie's Beauty Shop, Kelley's Beauty Shop, Alma's Beauty Shop, Yarbro's Beauty Shop, Joe's TV Repair, Butler's TV Service, Scotts Watch Repair, Decaturville Pool Room, Flower Basket, Flowers By Joyce, Wallace Welding and Sign Painting, City Wash, Martin's Machine Shop, and Davis Plumbing and Heating.

Parsons

The largest town in Decatur County is Parsons. Located near the center of the county, five miles west of the Tennessee River on state Highways 20, 100, and 69, it was first known as Parsons Flat. The site for Parsons was donated in 1889 by Henry Myracle. In order to get a town started on his land, he deeded 143 ⅓ acres to the Tennessee Midland Railroad Company on April 11, 1889.

The land was divided into lots with Myracle keeping every other row, which not only made money for him, but also promoted the growth of the new town. The town received its name from a Dock Parsons, presumedly son-in-law of Henry Myracle.

The chief road builder in the young town was L. H. Burke, who laid out Tennessee Avenue, 100 feet wide through the business section. His idea stemmed from assisting Captain Rae in laying out Pennsylvania Avenue in Washington, D.C. Main Street and all other streets in South Parsons were laid out at this time; however, North Parsons was not laid out until later.

The town was chartered in 1913 by an act of the general assembly. Instrumental in this action was G. W. Partin, who with other businessmen, realized the need for charter. He contacted Acklee Lancaster, a Lexington lawyer, who drew up the bill. A mayor had to be named rather than elected in the initial plans, so

Parsons, 1905. *Left to right:* Joe Wheat Mercantile, Mitchell Gibson's Jewelry Store, Tom Hayes General Mercantile, Tulane Hotel with G. W. Partin and Co. Mercantile on first floor, Bank of Parsons, Newt Arnold's Merchandise with Masonic Hall on second floor, Rains Hotel with B. F. Parlow business on first floor, Milton Houston Merchandise.

Will Neely, depot agent at that time, agreed to serve. Partin went to Nashville and presented the bill to Decatur and Benton County representative Joe Blount who introduced the bill in the general assembly. It passed and was signed by Governor Tom Rye.

Besides Will Neely, others serving as mayor of Parsons were T. P. Bateman, Carl W. Partin, J. J. Wesson, W. H. Partin, Arthur Tolley, Roy Garrett, Herman Rains, J. Madison Scott, Bob White, Parce Collett, Hobart Goff, Will Long, A. N. Graves, J. L. Lancaster, and Tim Boaz. Parce Collett was the youngest mayor in the town's history to date. He was 29 years old and served the 1960-1962 term in office. W. H. Neely served three terms, and Madison Scott is the only mayor to serve four terms. Tim Boaz is the incumbent mayor, having been elected June of 1976 to succeed J. L. Lancaster who served two terms.

The first aldermen were Frank Houston, Bob Laster, and Will Long. Other aldermen were A. N. Baugus, W. H. Neely, Jack Odle, Hobart Goff, J. D. Porter, J. E. Ingram, O. H. Roberts, N. J. Arnold, S. L. Jennings, J. J. Wesson, H. L. Beale, A. J. Hufstedler, Joe Jennings, G. C. Pollard, Paul Rains, Albert Bowman, L. F. Hufstedler, E. J. Houston, and F. J. Bray. Serving as aldermen in 1976 were Danny Roberts, vice-mayor, Johnny White, Charles Dickerson, Ab Price, Ronald Wart Dickson, James E. Wood, and W. B. Moore.

John Young served as the first city judge of Parsons and Lillye Younger served as the first female city judge succeeding Young in 1972. In 1976 Madison Scott was appointed city judge. Filling the office of recorder have been S. L. Jennings, Hurst Jennings, G. D. Long, Joe Crawley, Olan Davis, John Young, Nell Rogers, and Charlie Pratt. Leo Yarbro is serving as city manager having succeeded Buddy Yates.

Jim Averett was the first town marshall followed by W. E. Jordan, J. L. Lowe, Bud Anderson, J. W. Doyle, W. D. Bateman, R. F. Laster, J. M. Bateman, C. L. Hayes, W. D. Bateman, J. L. Lowe, Edward Brower, Spike Hayes, John Taylor, Jim Taylor, and A. R. Evans.

Originally John P. Rains Hotel and Mercantile.

Among the first business places in Parsons was a jewelry store operated by Mitchell Gibson. Pinkley Roberts ran the first mercantile store in the young town. William C. Cole owned the first telephone company. It was located in the back of Parsons Bank building, and Maude Arnold was the first telephone operator. T. P. Bateman was the second owner and operated it in his home on Eighth Street in Parsons. Later, Jack Odle bought the company and located it in the upstairs of Maxwell's Department Store, 105 Tennessee Avenue South. He moved it later into his home at the corner of North Main Street and Highway 69 North. After his death, his son, Dave Odle, continued the business independently until he sold it to Continental Telephone Company on January 19, 1966. The new dial system invaded Decatur County on April 28, 1953.

Perhaps the first hotel in Parsons was known as the Hop Steed Hotel. It was located on Florida Avenue just back of the Carl Partin house. At the death of Steed, the hotel was sold to Harrison Rains, who continued to run it.

A showplace for Parsons at the turn of the century was the Tulane Hotel on Main Street. The two-story brick structure was built by George Washington Partin who came to Decatur County from Ringo, Georgia. Ike Buckner was the contractor, and Horace White was the brickmason. Completed in 1896, the 12-room hotel was operated by Mr. and Mrs. Will Warden.

Partin ran a hardware store in the lower east side of the hotel building. On the west side was the hotel lobby, a dining area, which seated 50 persons, and the manager's living quarters. The rooms upstairs were for hotel use.

It received its name from the Tulane Hotel in Nashville. Partin stayed at the Nashville hotel and was so impressed that he asked the owners if he might use the name for his new hotel and was granted permission. The upstairs parlor was where Partin entertained dignitaries such as Governor Ben Hooper and Governor Alf Taylor. The elaborate furnishings came from Chicago.

Another showplace in the town was a hotel built by John P. Rains. The two-story, brick building was completed in 1898. Upon completion, a gala ball was held before furnishings were added. Downstairs quarters were used for a business place in which the owner operated a mercantile store. Three downstairs rooms were used for a lobby, dining area, and kitchen. There was a side entrance to the hotel. The upstairs was used for a hotel with the exception of three rooms which were used for the family.

Located at 600 Tennessee Avenue South, the second oldest brick house in Parsons was built for Jim Lamping in the early 1900s.

   Rains sold the building to the Colwick family and moved to
Memphis. Later W. D. Colwick and son, Glennie, bought the
business and continued operation of both the hotel and mercantile company. The hotel operation ceased, but the mercantile
business continued until 1972.

   Located at the intersection of Main Street and Tennessee
Avenue, the hotel had an iron-fenced garden with benches. In
later years, this was used for checker players in the town, and old
timers swapped yarns and knives.

Checker players in Colwick's yard, Parsons. *Front left to right:* Gene
Washburn, Joe Jordan; *rear left to right:* Ollie Hill, Obie Wilkins,
Hurlot Thomas.

The first bank located in Parsons was known as the Bank of Parsons, which was organized by L. H. Burke and Wid Long around 1903. This bank was located on Main Street in a two-story building. The first cashier was Leslie Rains. Its capital stock was $25,000. As was often the case during depression days, this bank was not able to re-open after President Franklin Roosevelt closed all banks. It was closed in 1931.

Farmers Bank opened its door for business in a side room of Milton Houston General Merchandise Building. The charter was obtained on April 15, 1907, and the bank was capitalized at $20,000. The original stockholders were John H. Jennings, Joe Jennings, W. W. Jennings, S. L. Jennings, Hiram Jennings, Ezra Jennings, Frank Houston, Dr. A. Y. Fisher, Joe Wheat, M. L. Houston, and D. W. Lacy. The first depositor was Mossie Arnold, who deposited ten cents.

In December of 1944 the bank reached a milestone in operation with total assets of one million dollars. With continued growth and after two additons to the old bank quarters, the directors decided to construct a new building. Located at 121 Tennessee Avenue South it opened for business April 7, 1954.

Another financial institution, Citizens State Bank, opened in Parsons on August 31, 1968. The bank was capitalized at $400,000 and had 204 stockholders. The initial board of directors included E. E. Mooney, Robert Fisher, Richard Charlton, Mrs. H. E. Barnett, Madison Scott, James Goff, Bud Tuten, Ralph Smith, James Smith, James Jordan, George A. Bell, J. C. Richardson, Carl McNeil, and Douglas Hayes. The bank moved into a modern new building in 1969 at 115 Main Street.

C. V. and Mae Maxwell started the first variety store in Parsons in 1927. It was located in a small building on Tennessee Avenue South and later moved to 105 Tennessee Avenue South. For a time tin dishpans were used for a cash register and at the close of the first day, the 5-10-25¢ items had reached the gigantic sum of $258. It took quite a time to count it out. Serving as clerks on opening day were K. K. and Mable Houston. It was the first store of its kind in Henderson, Perry, and Decatur counties.

First variety store in Decatur County.

Moviegoers in Parsons have been exposed to the entertainment for a long time. Showing silent movies, the first theater was located at 117-118 Tennessee Avenue South. It was a big tent owned and operated by a Mr. Drake in 1918 and 1919.

Later Jim Lamping operated a silent movie theater at 213 Tennessee Avenue South. It was a long wood building with individual seats. Between scenes entertainment was furnished by Mary Bruce Elvington, who played the piano.

Herman Rains operated a theater in the 1920s. He sold it to Hobart Goff who added an extension to the building where boxing matches were held. Among early fighters were Ray Dodson, Howard Greenway, Mutt Cagle, and others from Lexington and Jackson.

On Friday, November 26, 1971, the Perryville Post Office was closed. Velma Bibbs, officer in charge at the post office, took the American flag down. The last thing to come down was the sign "Perryville Post Office," thus leaving the once thriving river town as a village.

Beacon

Beacon, a town of about 150 citizens, four miles west of Parsons, was first known as "Moray." When the Tennessee Midland Railroad Company line came through Decatur County, the name of the town was changed to Beacon.

Mercantile operators in Beacon have been Jess Long, Will Dodd, Ike Smith, Chess Myracle, C. C. Thomas, Aussie Duke, and Glen Tolley, who has the only mercantile business operating now. Charley Thomas and Jess Long operated two cotton gins and blacksmith shops. Grist mills were run by Jim Bartholomew and Riley Hobbs. Beacon also had a saw mill which was operated by Jess Long. Bill O'Guinn owned the home telephone company and telephone operators at one time were Ethel Hayes and her sister, Carrie Hayes. Pink Lewis operated a barber shop and John Douglas was proprietor of a cafe at one time. Aaron Bartholomew also barbered there in the 1930s. When Highway 20 was constructed bypassing Beacon, business moved to the highway, and Beacon Junction was born.

A tragic event occurred on March 16, 1942, when Beacon was partially destroyed by a tornado. On that afternoon at about 4:20 darkness covered the area and as far as Parsons the sky turned a lemon yellow. When the tornado hit, the homes were twisted like a rope and bits of tin roofing were found miles away. Although Beacon was left in shambles, there was only one casualty, Bill O'Quinn.

Early settlers of Beacon include the Chumneys, Wallaces, Longs, Hayes, McCormicks, Douglases, O'Guinns, Keens, and Myracles. One very important person, Henry Myracle, founder of Parsons, is buried in an old cemetery in Beacon.

A great educational advantage to Decatur County was when the Parsons Public Library became a reality. The project began in 1963 when Lerah Washam and Lillye Younger, representing civic-minded groups in the community, proposed to Mayor Madison Scott that the town pay one-half of the cost of maintaining a public library. County court members voted to pay the other half of the cost.

Black settlers living in Parsons settled in an area called "Two Foot." An A.M.E. church was established and later business places located there. One such was Need-More, Sam Booty's store, located on South Georgia Avenue during the Depression days which furnished the settlement with groceries. Later a tea room opened, operated by Lynn Ray Scott and later by Gene Scott. Parham's Funeral Home located in Two Foot for a few years but moved later to Lexington.

Among the early settlers of Two Foot were Edd Clay, who was an early church leader. He had a son named Charley Clay who worked for G. W. Partin. Others were Guy Williams, who was employed at Holcomb Produce Company, Henry Fisher, who worked at Partin's Flour Mill, Square Faulkner, Henry Scott, Pete McDonald, Jim McElrath, Wes Ashcraft, who was highly respected and the father of Grant Ashcraft, and Henry McLemore.

Partinville

A forerunner of the town of Parsons was Partinville. A youthful, adventurous sewing machine salesman, George Washington Partin of Ringo, Georgia, was attracted by the natural advantages of the high land near Bear Creek. Believing there would be a profit in starting a town there, he purchased a number of acres near the present Bear Creek Baptist Church. After marrying Maggie Rushing, he opened a successful general merchandise store. He sold some of his land to Hop Steed who put up a cotton gin. Samuel Houston owned a cotton gin there also.

Since there was no post office nearby at this time, G. W. Partin made application for one. On November 13, 1885, he became the first postmaster in the town which bore his name. He served the office from November 13, 1885, until March 31, 1893, when John S. Barham became postmaster. However, a few years earlier a small settlement named Parsons had developed nearby. Being on the Midland Railroad, it grew faster and on May 7, 1897, the post office moved to Parsons. Partin sold his store and possessions at Partinville and also moved to the thriving new town in 1889. Some of the pioneer families living in the Partinville area were the Bostics, Steeds, Partins, Houstons, Lowes, Edwards, Meggs, Stegalls, Gilberts, Hayes, Myracles, Barnettes, and Iveys.

Perryville

Perryville, the oldest town in Decatur County, was incorporated before the county was organized. It was formerly a part of Perry County. Located on the Tennessee River, five miles east of Parsons, it was selected for the county seat of Perry County in 1821 by an act of the legislature. Charles Miles, John Rasser, James Dickson, Charles Graham, W. S. Britt, and William Patterson were appointed to locate the seat. The town was incorporated in 1825. Before being named Perryville, it was known as Midtown Community. Serving on the town board were Joseph Brown, William Jarman, J. S. Allen, J. W. Crowder, Jacob Johnson, James Kolough, and John McClover.

One of the first merchants in the thriving little river town was Samuel McClure. James M. and Curry Pettigrew of Armagh, Ireland, came to Perryville in 1825 and ran a mercantile business. They located branch stores in Decaturville, Oak Grove, Spring Creek in Madison County, and Beardstown in Perry County. William Stout, native of Forfar County, Scotland, met the Pettigrews while on a pleasure trip to this country and joined them in business. He later sold his business interests in Perryville and moved to Decaturville.

The railroad, which was laid from Memphis to Perryville, spawned new business places in the town. Two wholesale houses, Holcomb Produce Company and Shaw's Produce House, were

started. W. R. Dennison built the Dennison Hotel in 18[...] and Mrs. Henry Teague kept travelers in their home. [...] stores that emerged because of the railroad were John Add[...] Readey's Grocery, later operated by his sons, Jess and[...] Readey, John Young's Grocery, Knight Brothers Grocery,[...] MacMurray's Grocery, and Lemuel Rickman's Grocery. Ge[...] merchandise stores were also established. These included St[...] and Blount Company, L. M. Hearst General Merchandise,[...] Cole Brothers Store.

The old town of Perryville folded when Gilbertsville Dam[...] built. The business places and some houses were flooded. M[...] chants sold out, some quit, and the Readeys moved th[...] business to Parsons.

When the land was flooded lakes were formed, thus providi[...] a haven for sportsmen. In 1944 the Perryville Marina Boat Doc[...] was built by Doc Burton. Located in what was once a smal[...] branch, but now a large lake formed by the dam, it is the deepes[...] indentation along this area.

Perryville Marina.

Bible Hill

In the northern part of Decatur County, four miles east of the Henderson County line, lies the settlement of Bible Hill. At one time, there was a cotton gin, blacksmith shop, grist mill, stave mill, post office, two churches, a school, a doctor's office, and a big mercantile store located there.

The post office was established September 25, 1876, and R. M. Brown served as first postmaster. Wid and Hood Long operated a general store there in the early days and at that time the post office was located in one corner of the store. The Longs also operated a cotton gin, which was moved from Sulphur Fork. The general store was sold later to Robert Brown, an early doctor, whose two sons, Milt and John, operated it.

Early settlers included the Frizzells, Smiths, Jennings, Boxes, Patricks, Bakers, Fiddlers, Gulledges, Longs, Pettigrews, Hendrixes, Rubbs, Hamiltons, Haggards, Rains, MacMurrys, Taylors, Perrys, Browns, Stills, Dukes, Arnolds, and Dodsons.

Stave mill, 1896.

Sugar Tree

Sugar Tree, located in the northern corner of Decatur County, is 12 miles from Parsons. It received its name from the sugar maple trees that lined one side of the main street.

One of the early business places in the thriving, unincorporated town was Fry and Wesson General Mercantile, which carried everything from hair pins to horse collars. A small drug store was located at Sugar Tree where doctors came to fit glasses and make teeth. They built the town's hotel, which was operated by Wylie Coble and Joe Odle. Nattie Fisher kept boarders also. Blacksmiths were Jack Bates, Dol Spence, Tom Bates, John Farlow, and Bill Terry, whose blacksmith shop was located beneath a big sugar maple tree.

Another thriving business was the tobacco factory, owned by Nathaniel A. Wesson. A big two-story barn was used to smoke the tobacco leaves. A cotton gin was operated by Arthur Odle who also operated a mercantile business. A stave mill was also in operation for a while. Staves were transported to Ledbetter's Landing by oxen-drawn wagons. Hugh Cox was one of the drivers.

A brass band was organized and received much publicity. It was drawn by a wagon and team and the uniformed band members presented a colorful show. They made personal appearances on Children's Day at Wesson Chapel Cumberland Presbyterian Church and Cantrell Chapel Church of Christ just across the line in Benton County. Hal Fry was the drummer and others in the band were Dick Walker, Dock Odle, Joe Odle, Ernest Fry, John McLin, Dude Odle, Erie Wesson, Claude Spence, Joe Spence, and Bud Spence. To finance the band, box suppers and other fund drives were launched.

At one time Sugar Tree boasted a college, located on the present school ground. Among some of its early teachers were Dub Wesson, Zack Amerson, Nattie Fisher, Stella Britt, Zeda Fowler, Opal Odle, Mike Spence, Mel Tucker, and Bess Wesson. Later, there were 60 students taught by one teacher.

Bath Springs

Nestled in the southern hills of the extreme eastern portion of West Tennessee is Bath Springs, a community with a rich heritage. The town was named by Dr. William Hancock, who settled there and discovered the sulphur water, built a health resort, and named the little town Bath Springs. His medical office also served as a post office in pioneer days. Letters and packages were left for the people in the community.

In pre-Civil War days, a tanning factory operated in Bath Springs. The business was two-fold. The bark of trees was purchased to make acid to tan the hides. Cattle hides were tanned in the factory and shipped out by river boats. Bath Springs proper has no business places now, but four stores, a saw mill, and six churches are scattered over the nearby area.

One of the early families to locate in Bath Springs was the William Kindale family. Kindale was a veteran of the American Revolutionary War and lived to be 104 years of age. When the community was at its peak, it boasted 47 houses; however, there are only 21 houses there today, as people have left to find employment elsewhere.

Scotts Hill

Snuggled half in Decatur County and half in Henderson County lies the thriving town of Scotts Hill. It was in 1825 that Micajah Scott moved to Tennessee from North Carolina and settled at this locality. He opened the first store and the town was named in his honor. The old stage road ran through the town.

With the introduction of the stage coach came the post office service. The stage coach carried both passengers and mail. When the coach stopped, the passengers would alight and tour the town while the postmaster sorted the mail. A horn was sounded when the stage coach was ready to depart. Ephraim Austin was perhaps the first postmaster of Scotts Hill, and the post office was located in part of Austin's store.

The growing prosperity of the town was evidenced in 1906 when the Farmers State Bank was chartered. It had a capital stock of $10,000, a surplus of $8,000 and resources by 1929 of $175,000.

Misfortune hit the town twice in 1916. On May 17 of that year, a tornado swept the town, destroying the property and damaging the area. Again on October 16, an entire section of town was destroyed by fire. The blaze originated in the J. M. Brasher Store. Twelve stores, a barber shop, the I.O.O.F. Hall, blacksmith shop, cotton gin, post office, bank, hotel, and four residences were consumed by the flames.

Tornado or fire could not completely destroy Scotts Hill. The town was rebuilt and has extended its boundaries a distance of three miles. Extensions have been made on the Liberty and Stage Line Road as well as at Taylor's Crossing.

Since incorporation in the early 1900s, those who have served as mayor are Tom McKenzie, Acey Tarlton, Ellis Scott, J. E. Holland, Perry Murphy, H. T. Powers, Gordon Turner, and Wilson Miller.

Tie Whop

Tie Whop Community, located 12 miles south of Decaturville on Highway 69 between Turnbow and Stewman's creeks, received its name from an unusual circumstance. According to history a fisherman from Alabama floated down the Tennessee River in a houseboat and tied up at Garrett's Landing. One foggy night a steamboat came down the river and tied up at the landing. The fog was so dense the steamboat had to remain overnight. The big, husky fisherman bought a keg of whiskey from the boat, and friends and foes began consuming the "white lightning."

Soon a raucous battle began. The big fisherman was so strong that he would grab his opponent with a hold as they were tied up and then would "whop" him to the ground. It is told that one bystander remarked, "The old fisherman tied them up and whopped them over the head." The place became known as "Tie

Whop Bottom." Later, when the road came through the area, houses were built on the hill land near the bottom.

Lick Skillet

In the southwestern section of Decatur County is a community with an unusual name, Lick Skillet. In the early days, before streamlined highways, there was a lot of camping in nearby woods. The story goes that a group of campers cooked a big meal. One camper was late arriving and when he began to search for some food, all he found was the empty skillet. Being very hungry, he licked the skillet and from that day, the community has been known as Lick Skillet. A hill nearby is known as Pinkard Hill which was named for a Pinkard man who was hanged there. Settlers include the Montgomerys, Pattersons, Scates, Kelleys, Moodys, Clenneys, Ivys, Wyatts, and Averetts.

Cozette

In the early days a small settlement there was called Old Norford. Located ten miles north of Parsons, the community later changed its name to Cozette. At one time there was a blacksmith shop and grocery store. One of the early operators of the blacksmith shop was Lonnie Boyd, and Bunch Miller ran the general store. He also had a rolling store in which he traveled over the county in a truck stocked with goods.

The Oak Grove Cumberland Presbyterian Church and cemetery, as well as the Pentecostal Church also are part of the community. The Pentecostal Church is recent, but the Oak Grove Church dates back to a log church in pioneer days. After the log church a two-story structure was constructed which housed the Masonic Lodge and Eastern Star upstairs and church-school combination downstairs. Later a one-story, concrete block building was built which is still in use.

Decatur County Officials

Circuit Court Clerks

The first circuit court clerk was D. B. Funderburk who served until 1856, when he was succeeded by Hiram Lacy. Lacy held the office until 1860. Samuel Akin was then elected and held the office until the Civil War started. After the reorganization, C. S. Brandon and P. O. Roberts held the office until 1870 when D. M. Scott was elected and served the two following terms. J. P. Rains was elected to the office in 1878. P. W. Miller served from 1890 until 1894, when he was succeeded by Joe Jennings who served until 1898. John McMillan served in the office from 1900 until 1906. Marvin Spencer of Sugar Tree served from 1906 until 1910, at which time Bob Rhodes of Perryville took office and served until 1925; then W. V. Tucker of Decaturville was elected and served until 1930. Narcie Smith served in the office from 1930 to 1933 and Samuel L. Duck served from 1933 until 1941. Virgil Taylor was elected in 1941 and went out of office in 1950. He was succeeded by Albert Kindle. Floyd (Zeke) Graves was elected in 1958 and served until 1962 when Virgil Ray Box filled the office. He served from 1962 until 1970. He was succeeded by the present Circuit Court Clerk Charlie A. Kindle. Kindle is the great grandson of Hiram Lacy.

County Court Clerks

Serving as the first county court clerk in Decatur County was Samuel Yarbro, who was elected in 1846, at which time the first court was established in Decaturville. He served until 1856 and was succeeded by M. J. Fisher who served until 1860. J. R. Carmack served from 1860 until 1866. J. C. Roberts served from 1866 until 1868, and John P. Rains took office in 1868 and served until 1870. John McMillan served the office from 1870 until 1882 after which time J. E. Dees was elected and served until 1902. S.

L. Jennings filled the office from 1902 until 1906 and he was succeeded by Guy Yarbro who served from 1906 until 1910. O. H. Roberts served from 1910 until 1914 and P. H. Brasher took over from 1914 and served until 1922. C. C. Tubbs served from 1922 until 1923 at which time S. C. Kennedy served the office. He served from 1923 until 1934. R. Guy Butler filled the office from 1934 until 1942 and J. Madison Smith was elected in 1942 and served until 1946. B. B. Fisher was elected in 1946 and served until 1954 and he was succeeded by R. C. Montgomery whose term expired in 1978.

Decatur County Trustees

Those who have served as Decatur County Trustees since 1869 are as follows: 1869-1876, John Blount; 1876-1878, W. P. Bray; 1878-1884, John A. Long; 1884-1890, W. P. Miller; 1890-1896, J. T. Roberts; 1896-1902, J. J. Austin; 1902-1908, H. M. Johnson; 1908-1910, W. R. Johnson; 1910-1916, J. W. McIllwain; 1916-1918, W. L. Wheat; 1918-1923, Elbert Jones; 1923-1924, George L. Wortham, Sr.; 1924-1932, Will H. Duck; 1932-1936, Hobart Goff; 1936-1940, L. J. Thompson; 1940-1946, Jack Moore; 1946-1950, A. F. Hardin; 1950-1954, Clovis Pevahouse; 1954-1958, Jack Goff; 1958-1962, Alton M. Maners; 1962-1974, Hardin Smith; 1974—, and Janis W. McPeake.

Decatur County Registers

John A. Rains served as the county's first register in 1846 until 1848. He was followed by A. M. Yarbro who served from 1848 until 1857 at which time Samuel Brasher came into office and served until 1858. He was succeeded by William B. Bright who served from 1858 until 1863. J. G. W. Christenberry served the office from 1863 until 1864 and he was succeeded by William H. Milam who served from 1864 until 1866. John J. Lacy served from 1866 until 1870. William M. Pratt served the office from

1870 until 1882 when he was succeeded by T. R. Brasher who served from 1882 until 1886. G. B. D. Rushing served from 1886 until 1894 when he was succeeded by Jesse P. Veal who served from 1894 until 1897. J. W. Blount served from 1897 until 1898. R. W. Raney took office in 1898 and served until 1906 when he was succeeded by J. F. Adair who served from 1906 until 1918. Joe Tate succeeded him from 1918 until 1923. Mattie Tate filled the office from 1923 until 1926. Leonard O. Townsend served from 1926 until 1934. O. R. Houston served the office from 1934 until 1942 when he was succeeded by W. O. Baker who served from 1942 until 1950. Jimmy Fisher served from 1950 until 1954 and he was succeeded by Mrs. J. E. Ingram who served from 1954 until 1965. W. T. (Bill) Pomeroy was elected to this office in 1966 and is still serving.

Decatur County Judges

Decatur County judges serving from 1870 until 1976 are as follows: J. E. Brasher, 1870-1872; Houston Roberts, 1872-1882; C. A. Alston, 1882-1886; J. C. P. Myracle, 1886-1890; John W. Clift, 1890-1892; J. C. P. Myracle, 1892-1900; W. R. Tuten, 1900-1902; C. C. Lacy, 1902-1904; W. R. Tuten, 1904-1906; J. E. Dees, 1906-1910; H. A. Culp, 1910-1912; J. E. Dees, 1912-1914; J. A. England, 1914-1916; L. T. Smith, 1916-1918; J. M. Blount, 1918-1925; E. C. Kennedy, 1925-1934; Otto Milam, 1934-1950; Madison Smith, 1950-1957; Samuel L. Duck, 1957-1958; James Long, 1958-1959; Juanita Long, 1959-1974 (the first female county judge in Tennessee); and Hardin Smith, 1974 to the present.

General Session Judges

The first general session judge of Decatur County was Roy Stourt whose term of office began in 1960 and he served until 1963. He was followed by Grady Crawley whose term began in 1963 and he is still serving at this time.

Decatur County Tax Assessors

J. T. McMurray served from 1890 until 1892. He was succeeded by John Evans who began his term in 1892 and served until 1894. He was succeeded by J. A. Readey who served from 1908 until 1910. George Long served from 1912 until 1914. W. P. Davis served from 1916 until 1918. He was succeeded by A. G. Still who served from 1924 until 1928. G. W. Tucker served from 1928 until 1932. Meritt Cole served from 1932 until 1944 and he was succeeded by Oscar Douglas who served from 1944 until 1960. Sol Brasher served from 1960 until 1964. J. H. Austin was elected in 1964 and served until 1968. N. A. (Tony) Martin served the office from 1968 until 1972. He was succeeded by Jay Baker, whose term expires in 1980.

Clerks and Masters

D. B. Funderburk was appointed as clerk and master in 1845 and served until 1872 when D. C. Kennedy succeeded him and served from 1879 until 1887. He was succeeded by L. T. Smith who served from 1887 until 1894. P. W. Miller served from 1894 until 1923 and he was succeeded by Nelle Dunavant. In 1941 J. L. England took office and served until 1960 when Nell Tinker England was elected and is presently serving the office.

Sheriff

Decatur County's first sheriff was Hiram Lacy who served from 1846 until 1852 when Captain John McMillan took over and served until 1858. G. W. Haynes served from 1858 until 1862. He was succeeded by Benjaman Tuten from 1862 until 1866. J. C. Barnett served from 1866 until 1868. J. C. Houston served from 1868 until 1870. D. C. Kennedy served the office from 1870 until 1872. Isaiah McMillan filled the office from 1872 until 1874. W. R. Tuten served here from 1874 until 1876 when Isaiah McMillan served again from 1876 until 1882. E. E. Arnold served the office from 1882 until 1888. G. W. Boggan took over the office from 1888 until 1890. Joe Blount served from 1890 until 1896. Ben McMillan served from 1896 until 1898. J. M. Rains served from 1898 to 1900. In 1900 to 1904 the office was filled by George Brasher and W. E. Lancaster took over in 1904 and served until 1906. Joe Blount and Joe Odle served here from 1906 to 1910. From 1910 until 1914 the office was filled by Jim Chalk. J. A. Taylor succeeded him from 1914 until 1918. In 1918 Charley Beard was elected and served until 1924 when W. L. Wheat took over and served until 1928. Clayburn Hays served from 1928 until 1930. J. T. Odle filled the office from 1930 until 1934 when J. A. Taylor once again served the office until 1936. J. W. Conder served the office from 1936 until 1942. John Tolley served the office from 1942 until 1944. Again, J. W. Conder served here from 1944 until 1950 when J. B. Hayes filled the office until 1954. Carmon Montgomery served from 1954 until 1956 and he was followed by Ola Duck who held the office from 1956 until 1962. He was succeeded by Charlie Boroughs who served until 1968. Melvin Holland served the office from 1968 until 1970 when he was succeeded by J. K. Parrish who served until 1972. J. B. Dennison served the office from 1972 until 1976, at which time he was defeated by Ray Outlaw.

Road Commissioners

Serving Decatur County as road commissioners were F. E. H. Wood, Robert H. Fisher, and Dewey H. Anglin from 1942 until 1944. At this time, road commissioners were appointed by the county court to the various districts in the county. Colbert F. Moore, J. L. Hearington, and Henry W. Reed were appointed to serve in 1944. The law changed in 1945 and the legislature appointed the commissioners. Just prior to the appointment, Amsel DeLong served a short time. Dee Davis was the first one to serve as road supervisor. After his term the county appointed Adkins Maners in 1948. In 1950, the method was changed to election by popular vote.

Others elected were Oscar Lafferty, who served from 1952 until 1954, when he was succeeded by W. L. Renfroe. In 1956 Lafferty was re-elected and served continuously until 1962. H. P. (Booty) Long was elected in 1962 and was re-elected four times, the last term being 1970. John Wesley Smith was elected in 1970 and in 1972 he was re-elected. Long won the race in 1974 and is serving in the office presently.

The bench in Decatur County includes circuit court, chancery court, general sessions court, juvenile court, and city court. Representing the bar in the early history of the county were H. B. Neely, William S. Maxwell, W. F. Doherty, John McMillan, J. A. England, and D. E. Scott who are listed in *Goodspeeds* history. Among the other lawyers who have served are Benjamin Carlyle Welch, William Henry Fisher, Landon White, E. C. Kennedy, Samuel L. Duck, Vester Tucker, James Smith, Jim Smith, Edwin Townsend, Billy Townsend, Bob Townsend, Robert Livingston, Thomas B. Nunnerly, Henry Evans, Vernice Chumney, and James L. England.

Decatur Countians Serving in the Legislature

T. C. Taylor represented Decatur and Perry counties in the 32nd General Assembly from 1857 until 1859. Born in Williamson County in 1824, he was a farmer at Swallow Bluff. Marvin J. Fisher served the 34th General Assembly representing Decatur and Perry counties. He was the son of Jacob F. Fisher, a wealthy landowner in Decatur. Misfortune befell the legislator when he was killed in Decatur County in October of 1862 by Carroll Graves, reputedly over political differences. John Stegal, born in 1813, served as a legislator following Marvin J. Fisher, during Reconstruction days. Born in North Carolina, his name has been spelled variously as Stegald, Stegall and Steagall.

George W. Walters served the 37th General Assembly from 1871 until 1873 and represented Decatur and Perry counties.

Samuel W. Riggs served the 38th General Assembly, 1873 until 1875, representing Decatur and Hardin counties. G. W. Haynes served at the 40th General Assembly from 1877 until 1879, representing Decatur and Hardin counties. Born in Tennessee in 1822, he engaged in farming in Decaturville. H. B. Neeley served at the 42nd General Assembly, representing Decatur and Hardin counties. He died before the first extra session and the seat was filled by James D. Martin.

James J. Warren served at the 44th General Assembly, 1885 to 1887, representing Decatur, Lewis, and Perry counties. Born in Humphreys County, February 18, 1840, he was the son of Albert and Elizabeth Warren, natives of Virginia. He attended medical college at Louisville, Kentucky, and graduated in medicine in 1871 from the University of Nashville and practiced medicine at Bath Springs. John F. Akin served the 47th General Assembly, representing Decatur, Lewis, and Perry counties. Born January 1, 1838, he was a farmer and operated a grist mill and general store in Bath Springs.

Joseph M. Blount, member of the 54th General Assembly, represented Decatur and Benton counties. Born in Tennessee, November 26, 1858, son of John and Lucinda (Yarbro) Bount, he attended Decatur County schools, studied law and practiced in Decaturville. He began his career as a merchant and farmer, was sheriff of the county six years, elected road supervisor and election commissioner, and served as county judge.

James Tate Rogers served in the 56th General Assembly from 1909 until 1911, representing Decatur and Benton counties, and the 57th General Assembly from 1911 until his death representing Decatur, Benton, Hardeman, Hardin, and McNairy counties. Born in Henderson County, January 10, 1835, he was a Civil War veteran, and was wounded at the battle of Shiloh.

Benjamin Carlyle Welch served in the General Assemblies in 1917-1919 and 1921-1923, representing Decatur and Benton counties. Born at Decaturville, March 10, 1891, son of Pat H. and Nettie Welch, he attended the University of Tennessee and graduated in law from Cumberland University.

Jackson Landon White served in the 64th General Assembly, 1925-1927, representing Decatur and Benton counties. Born at Decaturville June 4, 1881, son of Robert Alexander and Fannie Dickerson White, he practiced law at Decaturville and served as circuit court clerk, county judge, postmaster, and secretary-treasurer of Decatur County National Farm Loan Association.

William Riley Thompson served the 66th General Assembly, 1929-1931, representing Decatur and Benton counties. Born at Cedar Creek in Perry County, December 26, 1859, he was the son of R. W. and Rebecca (Randal) Thompson.

James Earl Ingram served the 68th General Assembly, 1933-1935, representing Decatur and Benton counties. Born at Plattsburg, Mississippi in 1889, he began the practice of medicine in 1917 at Sugar Tree, Tennessee, and later moved to Parsons where he continued the practice until his death February 21, 1954.

Wilburn Branson Townsend served the 72nd and 82nd General Assemblies in 1941-1943 and 1961-1963, representing Decatur and Benton counties. Born in 1907 at Sugar Tree in the Hog Creek Community, son of Mansfield and Cordelia Estelle Harrison Townsend, he was an automobile dealer, insurance agent, and farmer. He was an alternate delegate in 1952 to the Democratic National Convention and delegate-at-large in 1960, chairman of the board of education, 1956, and co-manager in the 7th Congressional District for Edmund Orgill's candidacy for governor in the Democratic primary of 1958.

Hollis D. Pevahouse served in the 74th General Assembly, 1945-1947, representing Decatur and Benton counties. He was born in Wayne County October 17, 1899, son of Joseph Nelson and Ada Culp Pevahouse. He has served as president of Farmers Bank, and as chairman of the schoolboard in 1957 and lives in Decaturville.

Tim Boaz served in the 76th General Assembly, 1949-1951, representing Decatur and Benton counties. He was born at McKenzie in 1912, son of John J. and Clyde McCracken Boaz. Proprietor of Boaz Furnitue and Boaz Goodyear Tire Company, he served twice as mayor of Parsons.

Ernest E. Rhodes served the 78th and 89th General Assemblies, 1953-1955 and 1957-1959, representing Decatur and Benton counties. Born at Scotts Hill, February 4, 1910, son of Sam O. and Lily Thompson Rhodes, his occupations include merchant, farmer, and sawmill operator in Scotts Hill. He was elected justice of the peace in 1959 for the 10th Civil District.

G. L. Teague served the 88th General Assembly from 1972 until 1974. Born January 6, 1939, he lived in Henderson County, later moving to Parsons where he became engaged in the Ford dealership. He is the son of Mr. and Mrs. Earl Teague. During his term the counties represented were changed to Decatur, Perry, Wayne, and a portion of Lawrence and Hardin.

A Decatur Countian, who moved to Madison County and represented that county in the general assembly was Hobart L. Townsend who served the 70th and 71st General Assemblies, 1937-1941, representing Madison County. He was born at Sugar Tree, Decatur County, in August 1905, son of Eli Mansfield and Cordelia Harrison Townsend.

Decatur Countians Who Served in the Senate

William R. Tuten served in the 51st General Assembly of the Senate, 1899-1901, representing Decatur, Benton, and Humphreys counties. Born September of 1850, son of Benjamin F. and Hilda Tuten, he was a farmer at Bath Springs and served as justice of the peace from 1893 until 1898.

James K. Vise served the 71st General Assembly Senate, 1939-1941, representing Decatur, Benton, Hardeman, Hardin, and McNairy counties. Born at Vise Town September 10, 1897, son of E. M. and Lillian Thompson Vise, he has served as principal of Decatur County High School, and as county superintendent of schools.

Moss Arnold, first Decatur County historian.

Suggested Readings

Biographical Directory: Decatur County Members of the Tennessee General Assembly, 1796—.

Culp, Frederick M., and Mrs. Robert E. Ross. *Gibson County, Past and Present; The First General History of One of West Tennessee's Pivotal Counties.* Trenton: Gibson County Historical Society, 1961.

Dykeman, Wilma. *Tennessee A Bicentennial History.* New York, 1975.

Folmsbee, Stanley J., Corlew, Robert E., and Mitchell, Enoch L. *Tennessee: A Short History.* Knoxville: The University of Tennessee Press, 1969.

Goodspeed, Weston A., ed. "Decatur County." *History of Tennessee.* Nashville: Goodspeed Publishing Co., 1887. (Reprint, Southern Historical Press, Easley, S.C., 1978).

Greene, Lee S. and Avery, Robert S. *Government in Tennessee.* Knoxville: University of Tennessee Press, 1970.

Henry, Robert S. *"First with the Most" Forrest.* Indianapolis: Bobbs-Merrill, 1944.

Law, Harry L. *Tennessee Geography.* Chattanooga: Harlow Publishing Corporation, 1964.

Powers, Auburn. *History of Henderson County, Comprising an Account of the Facts Connected with the Early Settlement of the County; the Origin and the Development of the County; Slavery, the Civil War, and the Reconstruction Days; the World War and Present Conditions.* N.p.: n.p., 1930.

Smith, Sam. B. *Tennessee History: A Bibliography.* Knoxville: The University of Tennessee Press, 1974.

Tennessee Blue Book. Latest Edition, Nashville.

The West Tennessee Historical Society Papers. 33 Vols. 1947-1979.

Williams, Samuel Cole. *Early Travels in the Tennessee Country.* Johnson City, 1928.

_____. *The Beginnings of West Tennessee.* Johnson City, 1930.

Index

Lillye Washburn Younger was born on September 26, 1912, in Trenton, Tennessee, where she attended Peabody High School and Trenton Business College. Currently, she resides in Parsons, Tennessee, where she had worked as bookkeeper of Maxwell's Furniture Mart, and manager of Maxwell's Department Store. She is now serving as city judge and county historian.

In her capacity as historian, for 10 years she has presented a daily radio program on local history. She was society columnist for the Parsons' *New Leader* for 12 years and for 10 years, correspondent for the *Nashville Tennessean.* She had two books published: *People of Action* in 1969, and *History of Decatur County* in 1977.

Mrs. Younger, the wife of the late Harmon Joseph Younger of Paris, Tennessee, is an active member of the First Methodist Church, where she had taught teen and pre-teen Sunday school for 35 years. She had served also on the church administrative board as lay delegate to the annual conference, and as district officer for the United Methodist Women. She was a Parsons' girl scout leader for 16 years; a member of the West Tennessee Historical Society; the Peter Houston D.A.R.; the Nathan A. Wesson, U.D.C.; Parsons' Order of the Eastern Star; and Fidella's Garden Club.